STATUTORY SUPPLEMENT

CASES AND COMMENT

LABOR LAW

SECOND EDITION

by

STANLEY D. HENDERSON
F.D.G. Ribble Professor of Law Emeritus
University of Virginia

FOUNDATION PRESS
NEW YORK, NEW YORK
2005

© 2001 FOUNDATION PRESS
© 2005 By FOUNDATION PRESS
        395 Hudson Street
        New York, NY 10014
        Phone Toll Free 1–877–888–1330
        Fax (212) 367–6799
        fdpress.com
Printed in the United States of America

ISBN 1–58778–929–9

 TEXT IS PRINTED ON 10% POST CONSUMER RECYCLED PAPER

TABLE OF CONTENTS

*

STATUTORY SUPPLEMENT

CASES AND COMMENT

LABOR LAW

*

SELECTED STATUTES

SHERMAN ANTITRUST ACT

Act of July 2, 1890, 26 Stat. 209, as amended, 15 U.S.C. §§ 1–7

§ 1. Every contract, combination in the form of a trust or otherwise, or conspiracy, in restraint of trade or commerce among the several States, or with foreign nations, is hereby declared to be illegal. . . . Every person who shall make any contract or engage in any combination or conspiracy herein declared to be illegal shall be deemed guilty of a misdemeanor, and, on conviction thereof, shall be punished by fine not exceeding fifty thousand dollars, or by imprisonment not exceeding one year, or by both said punishments, in the discretion of the court.

§ 2. Every person who shall monopolize, or attempt to monopolize, or combine or conspire with any other person or persons, to monopolize any part of the trade or commerce among the several States, or with foreign nations, shall be deemed guilty of a misdemeanor, and, on conviction thereof, shall be punished by fine not exceeding fifty thousand dollars, or by imprisonment not exceeding one year, or by both said punishments, in the discretion of the court.

§ 3. Every contract, combination in form of trust or otherwise, or conspiracy, in restraint of trade or commerce in any Territory of the United States or of the District of Columbia, or in restraint of trade or commerce between any such Territory and another, or between any such Territory or Territories and any State or States or the District of Columbia, or with foreign nations, or between the District of Columbia and any State or States or foreign nations, is hereby declared illegal. Every person who shall make any such contract or engage in any such combination or conspiracy, shall be deemed guilty of a misdemeanor, and, on conviction thereof, shall be punished by fine not exceeding fifty thousand dollars, or by imprisonment not exceeding one year, or by both said punishments, in the discretion of the court.

§ 4. The several district courts of the United States are invested with jurisdiction to prevent and restrain violations of this act; and it shall be the duty of the several United States attorneys, in their respective districts, under the direction of the Attorney General, to institute proceedings in equity to prevent and restrain such violations. Such proceedings may be by way of petition setting forth the case and praying that such violation shall be enjoined or otherwise prohibited. When the parties complained of shall have been duly notified of such petition the court shall proceed, as soon as may be, to the hearing and determination of the case; and pending such petition and before final decree, the court may at any time make such temporary restraining order or prohibition as shall be deemed just in the premises.

§ 5.   Whenever it shall appear to the court before which any proceeding under section 4 of this title may be pending, that the ends of justice require that other parties should be brought before the court, the court may cause them to be summoned, whether they reside in the district in which the court is held or not; and subpoenas to that end may be served in any district by the marshal thereof.

§ 6.   Any property owned under any contract or by any combination, or pursuant to any conspiracy (and being the subject thereof) mentioned in section 1 of this act, and being in the course of transportation from one State to another, or to a foreign country, shall be forfeited to the United States, and may be seized and condemned by like proceedings as those provided by law for the forfeiture, seizure, and condemnation of property imported into the United States contrary to law. . . .

§ 8.   The word "person," or "persons," wherever used in this act shall be deemed to include corporations and associations existing under or authorized by the laws of either the United States, the laws of any of the Territories, the laws of any State, or the laws of any foreign country.

CLAYTON ANTITRUST ACT

Act of October 15, 1914, 38 Stat. 730, as amended, 15 U.S.C. §§ 12–31

Be it enacted by the Senate and House of Representatives of the United States of America in Congress Assembled, That "antitrust laws," as used herein, includes the Act entitled "An Act to protect trade and commerce against unlawful restraints and monopolies," approved July second, eighteen hundred and ninety [The Sherman Act]....

§ 6. That the labor of a human being is not a commodity or article of commerce. Nothing contained in the antitrust laws shall be construed to forbid the existence and operation of labor, agricultural, or horticultural organizations, instituted for the purposes of mutual help, and not having capital stock or conducted for profit, or to forbid or restrain individual members of such organizations from lawfully carrying out the legitimate objects thereof; nor shall such organizations, or the members thereof, be held or construed to be illegal combinations or conspiracies in restraint of trade, under the antitrust laws....

§ 16. That any person, firm, corporation, or association shall be entitled to sue for and have injunctive relief, in any court of the United States having jurisdiction over the parties, against threatened loss or damage by a violation of the antitrust laws, including sections 2, 3, 7 and 8 of this Act, when and under the same conditions and principles as injunctive relief against threatened conduct that will cause loss or damage is granted by courts of equity, under the rules governing such proceedings, and upon the execution of proper bond against damages for an injunction improvidently granted and a showing that the danger of irreparable loss or damage is immediate, a preliminary injunction may issue: *Provided,* That nothing herein contained shall be construed to entitle any person, firm, corporation, or association, except the United States, to bring suit in equity for injunctive relief against any common carrier subject to the provisions of the Act to regulate commerce, approved February fourth, eighteen hundred and eighty-seven, in respect of any matter subject to the regulation, supervision, or other jurisdiction of the Interstate Commerce Commission....

§ 20. That no restraining order or injunction shall be granted by any court of the United States, or a judge or the judges thereof, in any case between an employer and employees, or between employers and employees, or between employees, or between persons employed and persons seeking employment, involving, or growing out of, a dispute concerning terms or conditions of employment, unless necessary to prevent irreparable injury to property, or to a property right, of the party making the application, for which injury there is no adequate remedy at law, and such property or property right must be described with particularity in the application, which must be in writing and sworn to by the applicant or by his agent or attorney.

And no such restraining order or injunction shall prohibit any person or persons, whether singly or in concert, from terminating any relation of employment, or from ceasing to perform any work or labor, or from recommending, advising, or persuading others by peaceful and lawful means so to do; or from attending at any place where any such person or persons may lawfully be, for the purpose of peacefully obtaining or communicating information, or from peacefully persuading any person to work or to abstain from working; or from ceasing to patronize or to employ any party to such dispute, or from recommending, advising, or persuading others by peaceful and lawful means to do; or from paying or giving to, or withholding from, any person engaged in such dispute, any strike benefits or other moneys or things of value; or from peaceably assembling in a lawful manner, and for lawful purposes; or from doing any act or thing which might lawfully be done in the absence of such dispute by any party thereto; nor shall any of the acts specified in this paragraph be considered or held to be violations of any law of the United States.

NORRIS–LaGUARDIA ACT

Act of March 23, 1932, 47 Stat. 70 (1932), 29 U.S.C. §§ 101–115

Be it enacted by the Senate and House of Representatives of the United States of America in Congress Assembled, That no court of the United States, as herein defined, shall have jurisdiction to issue any restraining order or temporary or permanent injunction in a case involving or growing out of a labor dispute, except in a strict conformity with the provisions of this Act; nor shall any such restraining order or temporary or permanent injunction be issued contrary to the public policy declared in this Act.

§ 2. In the interpretation of this Act and in determining the jurisdiction and authority of the courts of the United States, as such jurisdiction and authority are herein defined and limited, the public policy of the United States is hereby declared as follows:

Whereas under prevailing economic conditions, developed with the aid of governmental authority for owners of property to organize in the corporate and other forms of ownership association, the individual unorganized worker is commonly helpless to exercise actual liberty of contract and to protect his freedom of labor, and thereby to obtain acceptable terms and conditions of employment, wherefore, though he should be free to decline to associate with his fellows, it is necessary that he have full freedom of association, self-organization, and designation of representatives of his own choosing, to negotiate the terms and conditions of his employment, and that he shall be free from the interference, restraint, or coercion of employers of labor, or their agents, in the designation of such representatives or in self-organization or in other concerted activities for the purpose of collective bargaining or other mutual aid or protection; therefore, the following definitions of and limitations upon the jurisdiction and authority of the courts of the United States are hereby enacted.

§ 3. Any undertaking or promise, such as is described in this section, or any other undertaking or promise in conflict with the public policy declared in section 2 of this Act is hereby declared to be contrary to the public policy of the United States, shall not be enforceable in any court of the United States and shall not afford any basis for the granting of legal or equitable relief by any such court, including specifically the following:

Every undertaking or promise hereafter made, whether written or oral, express or implied, constituting or contained in any contract or agreement of hiring or employment between any individual, firm, company, association, or corporation, and any employee or prospective employee of the same whereby

(a) Either party to such contract or agreement undertakes or promises not to join, become, or remain a member of any labor organization or of any employer organization; or

(b) Either party to such contract or agreement undertakes or promises that he will withdraw from an employment relation in the event that he joins, becomes, or remains a member of any labor organization or of any employer organization.

§ 4. No court of the United States shall have jurisdiction to issue any restraining order or temporary or permanent injunction in any case involving or growing out of any labor dispute to prohibit any person or persons participating or interested in such dispute (as these terms are herein defined) from doing, whether singly or in concert, any of the following acts:

(a) Ceasing or refusing to perform any work or to remain in any relation of employment;

(b) Becoming or remaining a member of any labor organization or of any employer organization, regardless of any such undertaking or promise as is described in section 3 of this Act;

(c) Paying or giving to, or withholding from, any person participating or interested in such labor dispute any strike or unemployment benefits or insurance, or other moneys or things of value;

(d) By all lawful means aiding any person participating or interested in any labor dispute who is being proceeded against in, or is prosecuting, any action or suit in any court of the United States or of any State;

(e) Giving publicity to the existence of, or the facts involved in, any labor dispute, whether by advertising, speaking, patrolling, or by any other method not involving fraud or violence;

(f) Assembling peaceably to act or to organize to act in promotion of their interests in a labor dispute;

(g) Advising or notifying any person of an intention to do any of the acts heretofore specified;

(h) Agreeing with other persons to do or not to do any of the acts heretofore specified; and

(i) Advising, urging, or otherwise causing or inducing without fraud or violence the acts heretofore specified, regardless of any such undertaking or promise as is described in section 3 of this Act.

§ 5. No court of the United States shall have jurisdiction to issue a restraining order or temporary or permanent injunction upon the ground that any of the persons participating or interested in a labor dispute constitute or are engaged in an unlawful combination or conspiracy because of the doing in concert of the acts enumerated in section 4 of this Act.

§ 6. No officer or member of any association or organization, and no association or organization participating or interested in a labor dispute, shall be held responsible or liable in any court of the United States for the unlawful acts of individual officers, members, or agents, except upon clear proof of actual participation in, or actual authorization of, such acts, or of ratification of such acts after actual knowledge thereof.

§ 7. No court of the United States shall have jurisdiction to issue a temporary or permanent injunction in any case involving or growing out of a labor dispute, as herein defined, except after hearing the testimony of witnesses in open court (with opportunity for cross-examination) in support of the allegations of a complaint made under oath, and testimony in opposition thereto, if offered, and except after findings of fact by the court, to the effect—

(a) That unlawful acts have been threatened and will be committed unless restrained or have been committed and will be continued unless restrained, but no injunction or temporary restraining order shall be issued on account of any threat or unlawful act excepting against the person or persons, association, or organization making the threat or committing the unlawful act or actually authorizing or ratifying the same after actual knowledge thereof;

(b) That substantial and irreparable injury to complainant's property will follow;

(c) That as to each item of relief granted greater injury will be inflicted upon complainant by the denial of relief than will be inflicted upon defendants by the granting of relief;

(d) That complainant has no adequate remedy at law; and

(e) That the public officers charged with the duty to protect complainant's property are unable or unwilling to furnish adequate protection.

Such hearing shall be held after due and personal notice thereof has been given, in such manner as the court shall direct, to all known persons against whom relief is sought, and also to the chief of those public officials of the county and city within which the unlawful acts have been threatened or committed charged with the duty to protect complainant's property: *Provided, however,* That if a complainant shall also allege that, unless a temporary restraining order shall be issued without notice, a substantial and irreparable injury to complainant's property will be unavoidable, such a temporary restraining order may be issued upon testimony under oath, sufficient, if sustained, to justify the court in issuing a temporary injunction upon a hearing after notice. Such a temporary restraining order shall be effective for no longer than five days and shall become void at the expiration of said five days. No temporary restraining order or temporary injunction shall be issued except on condition that complainant shall first file an undertaking with adequate security in an amount to be fixed by the court sufficient to recompense those enjoined for any loss, expense, or damage caused by the improvident or erroneous issuance of such order or injunction, including all reasonable costs (together with a reasonable attorney's fee) and expense of defense against the order or against the granting of any injunctive relief sought in the same proceeding and subsequently denied by the court.

The undertaking herein mentioned shall be understood to signify an agreement entered into by the complainant and the surety upon which a decree may be rendered in the same suit or proceeding against said complainant and surety, upon a hearing to assess damages of which hearing complainant and surety shall have reasonable notice, the said complainant and surety submitting themselves to the jurisdiction of the court for that purpose. But nothing herein contained shall deprive any party having a claim or cause of action under or upon such undertaking from electing to pursue his ordinary remedy by suit at law or in equity.

§ **8.**   No restraining order or injunctive relief shall be granted to any complainant who has failed to comply with any obligation imposed by law which is involved in the labor dispute in question, or who has failed to make every reasonable effort to settle such dispute either by negotiation or with the aid of any available governmental machinery of mediation or voluntary arbitration.

§ **9.**   No restraining order or temporary or permanent injunction shall be granted in a case involving or growing out of a labor dispute, except on the basis of findings of fact made and filed by the court in the record of the case prior to the issuance of such restraining order or injunction; and every restraining order or injunction granted in a case involving or growing out of a labor dispute shall include only a prohibition of such specific act or acts as may be expressly complained of in the bill of complaint or petition filed in such case and as shall be expressly included in said findings of fact made and filed by the court as provided herein.

§ **10.**   Whenever any court of the United States shall issue or deny any temporary injunction in a case involving or growing out of a labor dispute, the court shall, upon the request of any party to the proceedings and on his filing the usual bond for costs, forthwith certify as in ordinary cases the record of the case to the court of appeals for its review. Upon the filing of such record in the court of appeals, the appeal shall be heard and the temporary injunctive order affirmed, modified, or set aside with the greatest possible expedition, giving the proceedings precedence over all other matters except older matters of the same character. . . .

§ **13.**   When used in this Act, and for the purposes of this Act—

(a) A case shall be held to involve or to grow out of a labor dispute when the case involves persons who are engaged in the same industry, trade, craft, or occupation; or have direct or indirect interests therein; or who are employees of the same employer; or who are members of the same or an affiliated organization of employers or employees; whether such dispute is (1) between one or more employers or associations of employers and one or more employees or associations of employees; (2) between one or more employers or associations of employers and one or more employers or associations of employers; or (3) between one or more employees or associations of employees and one or more employees or associations of employees; or when the case involves any conflicting or competing interests in a "labor dispute" (as hereinafter defined) of "persons participating or interested" therein (as hereinafter defined).

(b) A person or association shall be held to be a person participating or interested in a labor dispute if relief is sought against him or it, and if he or it is engaged in the same industry, trade, craft, or occupation in which such dispute occurs, or has a direct or indirect interest therein, or is a member, officer, or agent of any association composed in whole or in part of employers or employees engaged in such industry, trade, craft, or occupation.

(c) The term "labor dispute" includes any controversy concerning terms or conditions of employment, or concerning the association or representation of persons in negotiating, fixing, maintaining, changing, or seeking to arrange terms or conditions of employment, regardless of whether or not the disputants stand in the proximate relation of employer and employee.

(d) The term "court of the United States" means any court of the United States whose jurisdiction has been or may be conferred or defined or limited by Act of Congress, including the courts of the District of Columbia.

§ 14. If any provision of this Act or the application thereof to any person or circumstance is held unconstitutional or otherwise invalid, the remaining provisions of the Act and the application of such provisions to other persons or circumstances shall not be affected thereby.

§ 15. All Acts and parts of Acts in conflict with the provisions of this Act are hereby repealed.

*

RAILWAY LABOR ACT

44 Stat. 577 (1926), as amended by 48 Stat. 1185 (1934), 49 Stat. 1189 (1936), 54 Stat. 785 (1940), 64 Stat. 1238 (1951), 78 Stat. 748 (1964), 80 Stat. 208 (1966); 45 U.S.C. §§ 151–188

TITLE I

DEFINITIONS

§ 1. When used in this Act and for the purposes of this Act—

First. The term "carrier" includes any express company, sleeping-car company, carrier by railroad, subject to the Interstate Commerce Act, and any company which is directly or indirectly owned or controlled by or under common control with any carrier by railroad and which operates any equipment or facilities or performs any service (other than trucking service) in connection with the transportation, receipt, delivery, elevation, transfer in transit, refrigeration or icing, storage, and handling of property transported by railroad, and any receiver, trustee, or other individual or body, judicial or otherwise, when in the possession of the business of any such "carrier": *Provided, however,* That the term "carrier" shall not include any street, interurban, or suburban electric railway, unless such railway is operating as a part of a general steam-railroad system of transportation, but shall not exclude any part of the general steam-railroad system of transportation now or hereafter operated by any other motive power. The Interstate Commerce Commission is authorized and directed upon request of the Mediation Board or upon complaint of any party interested to determine after hearing whether any line operated by electric power falls within the terms of this proviso. The term "carrier" shall not include any company by reason of its being engaged in the mining of coal, the supplying of coal to a carrier where delivery is not beyond the mine tipple, and the operation of equipment or facilities therefor, or in any of such activities.

Second. The term "Adjustment Board" means that National Railroad Adjustment Board created by this Act.

Third. The term "Mediation Board" means the National Mediation Board created by this Act.

Fourth. The term "commerce" means commerce among the several States or between any State, Territory, or the District of Columbia and any foreign nation, or between any Territory or the District of Columbia and any State, or between any Territory and any other Territory, or between any Territory and the District of Columbia, or within any Territory or the District of Columbia, or between points in the same State but through any other State or any Territory or the District of Columbia or any foreign nation.

Fifth. The term "employee" as used herein includes every person in the service of a carrier (subject to its continuing authority to supervise and direct the manner of rendition of his service) who performs any work defined as that of an employee or subordinate official in the orders of the Interstate Commerce Commission now in effect, and as the same may be amended or interpreted by orders hereafter entered by the Commission pursuant to the authority which is conferred upon it to enter orders amending or interpreting such existing orders: *Provided, however,* That no occupational classification made by order of the Interstate Commerce Commission shall be construed to define the crafts according to which railway employees may be organized by their voluntary action, nor shall the jurisdiction or powers of such employee organizations be regarded as in any way limited or defined by the provisions of this Chapter or by the orders of the Commission.

The term "employee" shall not include any individual while such individual is engaged in the physical operations consisting of the mining of coal, the preparation of coal, the handling (other than movement by rail with standard railroad locomotives) of coal not beyond the mine tipple, or the loading of coal at the tipple.

Sixth. The term "representative" means any person or persons, labor union, organization, or corporation designated either by a carrier or group of carriers or by its or their employees, to act for it or them.

Seventh. The term "district court" includes the United States District Court for the District of Columbia; and the term "court of appeals" includes the United States Court of Appeals for the District of Columbia.

GENERAL PURPOSES

§ 2. The purposes of the Act are: (1) To avoid any interruption to commerce or to the operation of any carrier engaged therein; (2) to forbid any limitation upon freedom of association among employees or any denial, as a condition of employment or otherwise, of the right of employees to join a labor organization; (3) to provide for the complete independence of carriers and of employees in the matter of self-organization to carry out the purposes of this chapter; (4) to provide for the prompt and orderly settlement of all disputes concerning rates of pay, rules, or working conditions; (5) to provide for the prompt and orderly settlement of all disputes growing out of grievances or out of the interpretation or application of agreements covering rates of pay, rules, or working conditions.

GENERAL DUTIES

First. It shall be the duty of all carriers, their officers, agents, and employees to exert every reasonable effort to make and maintain agreements concerning rates of pay, rules, and working conditions, and to settle all disputes, whether arising out of the application of such agreements or otherwise, in order to avoid any interruption to commerce or to the operation of any carrier growing out of any dispute between the carrier and the employees thereof.

Second. All disputes between a carrier or carriers and its or their employees shall be considered, and, if possible, decided, with all expedition, in conference between representatives designated and authorized so to confer, respectively, by the carrier or carriers and by the employees thereof interested in the dispute.

Third. Representatives, for the purposes of this Act, shall be designated by the respective parties without interference, influence, or coercion by either party over the designation of representatives by the other; and neither party shall in any way interfere with, influence, or coerce the other in its choice of representatives. Representatives of employees for the purposes of this Act need not be persons in the employ of the carrier, and no carrier shall, by interference, influence, or coercion seek in any manner to prevent the designation by its employees as their representatives of those who or which are not employees of the carrier.

Fourth. Employees shall have the right to organize and bargain collectively through representatives of their own choosing. The majority of any craft or class of employees shall have the right to determine who shall be the representative of the craft or class for the purposes of this Act. No carrier, its officers, or agents shall deny or in any way question the right of its employees to join, organize, or assist in organizing the labor organization of their choice, and it shall be unlawful for any carrier to interfere in any way with the organization of its employees, or to use the funds of the carrier in maintaining or assisting or contributing to any labor organization, labor representative, or other agency of collective bargaining, or in performing any work therefor, or to influence or coerce employees in an effort to induce them to join or remain or not to join or remain members of any labor organization, or to deduct from the wages of employees any dues, fees, assessments, or other contributions payable to labor organizations, or to collect or to assist in the collection of any such dues, fees, assessments, or other contributions: *Provided,* That nothing in this Act shall be construed to prohibit a carrier from permitting an employee, individually, or local representatives of employees from conferring with management during working hours without loss of time, or to prohibit a carrier from furnishing free transportation to its employees while engaged in the business of a labor organization.

Fifth. No carrier, its officers, or agents shall require any person seeking employment to sign any contract or agreement promising to join or not to join a labor organization; and if any such contract has been enforced prior to the effective date of this Act, then such carrier shall notify the employees by an appropriate order that such contract has been discarded and is no longer binding on them in any way.

Sixth. In case of a dispute between a carrier or carriers and its or their employees, arising out of grievances or out of the interpretation or application of agreements concerning rates of pay, rules, or working conditions, it shall be the duty of the designated representative or representatives of such carrier or carriers and of such employees, within ten days after the receipt of notice of a desire on the part of either party to confer in respect to such dispute, to specify a time and place at which such conference shall be held: *Provided,* (1) That the place so specified shall be situated upon the line of the carrier involved or as otherwise mutually agreed upon; and (2) that the time so specified shall allow the designated conferees reasonable opportunity to reach such place of conference, but shall not exceed twenty days from the receipt of such notice: *And provided further,* That nothing in this Act shall be construed to supersede the provisions of any agreement (as to conferences) then in effect between the parties.

Seventh. No carrier, its officers, or agents shall change the rates of pay, rules, or working conditions of its employees, as a class as embodied in agreements except in the manner prescribed in such agreements or in section 6 of this Act.

Eighth. Every carrier shall notify its employees by printed notices in such form and posted at such times and places as shall be specified by the Mediation Board that all disputes between the carrier and its employees will be handled in accordance with the requirements of this Act, and in such notices there shall be printed verbatim, in large type, the third, fourth, and fifth paragraphs of this section. The provisions of said paragraphs are hereby made a part of the contract of employment between the carrier and each employee, and shall be held binding upon the parties, regardless of any other express or implied agreements between them.

Ninth. If any dispute shall arise among a carrier's employees as to who are the representatives of such employees designated and authorized in accordance with the requirements of this Act, it shall be the duty of the Mediation Board, upon request of either party to the dispute, to investigate such dispute and to certify to both parties, in writing, within thirty days after the receipt of the invocation of its services, the name or names of the individuals or organizations that have been designated and authorized to represent the employees involved in the dispute, and certify the same to the carrier. Upon receipt of such certification the carrier shall treat with the representative so certified as the representative of the craft or class for the purposes of this Act. In such an investigation, the Mediation Board shall be authorized to take a secret ballot of the employees involved, or to utilize any other appropriate method of ascertaining the names of their duly designated and authorized representatives in such manner as shall insure the choice of representatives by the employees without interference, influence, or coercion exercised by the carrier. In the conduct of any election for the purposes herein indicated the Board shall designate who may participate in the election and establish the rules to govern the election, or may appoint a committee of three neutral persons who after hearing shall within ten days designate the employees who may participate in the election. The Board shall have access to and have power to make copies of the books and records of the carriers to obtain and utilize such information as may be deemed necessary by it to carry out the purposes and provisions of this paragraph.

Tenth. The willful failure or refusal of any carrier, its officers or agents, to comply with the terms of the third, fourth, fifth, seventh, or eighth paragraph of this section shall be a misdemeanor, and upon conviction thereof the carrier, officer, or agent offending shall be subject to a fine of not less than $1,000, nor more than $20,000, or imprisonment for not more than six months, or both fine and imprisonment, for each offense, and each day during which such carrier, officer, or agent shall willfully fail or refuse to comply with the terms of the said paragraphs of this section shall constitute a separate offense. It shall be the duty of any district attorney of the United States to whom any duly designated representative of a carrier's employees may apply to institute in the proper court and to prosecute under the direction of the Attorney General of the United States, all necessary proceedings for the enforcement of the provisions of this section, and for the punishment of all violations thereof and the costs and expenses of such prosecution shall be paid out of the appropriation for the expenses of the courts of the United States: *Provided,* That nothing in this Act shall be construed to require an individual employee to render labor or service without his consent, nor shall anything in this Act be construed to make the quitting of his labor by an individual employee an illegal act; nor shall any court issue any process to compel the performance by an individual employee of such labor or service, without his consent.

Eleventh. Notwithstanding any other provisions of this Act, or of any other statute or law of the United States, or Territory thereof, or of any State, any carrier or carriers as defined in this Act and a labor organization or labor organizations duly designated and authorized to represent employees in accordance with the requirements of this chapter shall be permitted—

(a) to make agreements, requiring, as a condition of continued employment, that within sixty days following the beginning of such employment, or the effective date of such agreements, whichever is the later, all employees shall become members of the labor organization representing their craft or class: *Provided,* That no such agreement shall require such condition of employment with respect to employees to whom membership is not available upon the same terms and conditions as are generally applicable to any other member or with respect to employees to whom membership was denied or terminated for any reason other than the failure of the employee to tender the periodic dues, initiation fees, and assessments (not including fines and penalties) uniformly required as a condition of acquiring or retaining membership.

(b) to make agreements providing for the deduction by such carrier or carriers from the wages of its or their employees in a craft or class and payment to the labor organization representing the craft or class of such employees, of any periodic dues, initiation fees, and assessments (not including fines and penalties) uniformly required as a condition of acquiring or retaining membership: *Provided,* That no such agreement shall be effective with respect to any individual employee until he shall have furnished the employer with a written assignment to the labor organization of such membership dues, initiation fees, and assessments, which shall be revocable in writing after the expiration of one year or upon the termination date of the applicable collective agreement, whichever occurs sooner....

(d) Any provisions in paragraphs Fourth and Fifth of section 2 of this Act in conflict herewith are to the extent of such conflict amended.

NATIONAL BOARD OF ADJUSTMENT—GRIEVANCES—INTERPRETATION OF AGREEMENTS

§ 3. **First.** There is hereby established a Board, to be known as the "National Railroad Adjustment Board," the members of which shall be selected within thirty days after approval of this Act, and it is hereby provided—

(a) That the said Adjustment Board shall consist of thirty-six members, eighteen of whom shall be selected by the carriers and eighteen by such labor organizations of the employees, national in scope, as have been or may be organized in accordance with the provisions of section 2 of this Act.

(b) The carriers, acting each through its board of directors or its receiver or receivers, trustee or trustees, or through an officer or officers designated for that purpose by such board, trustee or trustees, or receiver or receivers, shall prescribe the rules under which its representatives shall be selected and shall select the representatives of the carriers on the Adjustment Board and designate the division on which each such representative shall serve, but no carrier or system of carriers shall have more than one representative on any division of the Board.

(c) The national labor organizations, as defined in paragraph (a) of this section, acting each through the chief executive or other medium designated by the organization or association thereof, shall prescribe the rules under which the labor members of the Adjustment Board shall be selected and shall select such members and designate the division on which each member shall serve; but no labor organization shall have more than one representative on any division of the Board....

(h) The said Adjustment Board shall be composed of four divisions, whose proceedings shall be independent of one another, and the said divisions as well as the number of their members shall be as follows:

First division: To have jurisdiction over disputes involving train- and yard-service employees of carriers; that is, engineers, firemen, hostlers, and outside hostler helpers, conductors, trainmen, and yard-service employees. This division shall consist of ten members, five of whom shall be selected and designated by the carriers and four of whom shall be selected and designated by the labor organizations of the employees.

Second division: To have jurisdiction over disputes involving machinists, boilermakers, blacksmiths, sheet-metal workers, electrical workers, carmen, the helpers and apprentices of all the foregoing, coach cleaners, power-house employees, and railroad-shop laborers. This division shall consist of ten members, five of whom shall be selected by the carriers and five by the national labor organizations of the employees.

Third division: To have jurisdiction over disputes involving station, tower, and telegraph employees, train dispatchers, maintenance-of-way men, clerical employees, freight handlers, express, station, and store employees, signal men, sleeping-car conductors, sleeping-car porters, and maids and dining-car employees. This division shall consist of ten members, five of whom shall be selected by the carriers and five by the national labor organizations of employees.

Fourth division: To have jurisdiction over disputes involving employees of carriers directly or indirectly engaged in transportation of passengers or property by water, and all other employees of carriers over which jurisdiction is not given to the first, second, and third divisions. This division shall consist of six members, three of whom shall be selected by the carriers and three by the national labor organizations of the employees.

(i) The disputes between an employee or group of employees and a carrier or carriers growing out of grievances or out of the interpretation or application of agreements concerning rates of pay, rules, or working conditions, including cases pending and unadjusted on the date of approval of this Act, shall be handled in the usual manner up to and including the chief operating officer of the carrier designated to handle such disputes; but, failing to reach an adjustment in this manner, the disputes may be referred by petition of the parties or by either party to the appropriate division of the Adjustment Board with a full statement of the facts and all supporting data bearing upon the disputes....

(m) The awards of the several divisions of the Adjustment Board shall be stated in writing. A copy of the awards shall be furnished to the respective parties to the controversy, and the awards shall be final and binding upon both parties to the dispute. In case a dispute arises involving an interpretation of the award the division of the Board upon request of either party shall interpret the award, in the light of the dispute.

(n) A majority vote of all members of the division of the Adjustment Board shall be competent to make an award with respect to any dispute submitted to it.

(*o*) In case of an award by any division of the Adjustment Board in favor of petitioner, the division of the Board shall make an order, directed to the carrier, to make the award effective and, if the award includes a requirement for the payment of money, to pay the employee the sum to which he is entitled under the award on or before a day named. In the event any division determines that an award favorable to the petitioner should not be made in any dispute referred to it, the division shall make an order to the petitioner stating such determination.

(p) If a carrier does not comply with an order of a division of the Adjustment Board within the time limit in such order, the petitioner, or any person for whose benefit such order was made, may file in the District Court of the United States for the district in which he resides or in which is located the principal operating office of the carrier, or through which the carrier operates, a petition setting forth briefly the causes for which he claims relief, and the order of the division of the Adjustment Board in the premises. Such suit in the District Court of the United States shall proceed in all respects as other civil suits, except that on the trial of such suit the findings and order of the division of the Adjustment Board shall be conclusive on the parties, and except that the petitioner shall not be liable for costs in the district court nor for costs at any subsequent stage of the proceedings, unless they accrue upon his appeal, and such costs shall be paid out of the appropriation for the expenses of the courts of the United States. If the petitioner shall finally prevail he shall be allowed a reasonable attorney's fee, to be taxed and collected as a part of the costs of the suit. The district courts are empowered, under the rules of the court governing actions at law, to make such order and enter such judgment, by writ of mandamus or otherwise, as may be appropriate to enforce or set aside the order of the division of the Adjustment Board: *Provided, however,* That such order may not be set aside except for failure of the division to comply with the requirements of this Act, for failure of the order to conform, or confine itself, to matters within the scope of the division's jurisdiction, or for fraud or corruption by a member of the division making the order.

(q) If any employee or group of employees, or any carrier, is aggrieved by the failure of any division of the Adjustment Board to make an award in a dispute referred to it, or is aggrieved by any of the terms of an award or by the failure of the division to include certain terms in such award, then such employee or group of employees or carrier may file in any United States district court in which a petition under paragraph (p) could be filed, a petition for review of the division's order. A copy of the petition shall be forthwith transmitted by the clerk of the court to the Adjustment Board. The Adjustment Board shall file in the court the record of the proceedings on which it based its action. The court shall have jurisdiction to affirm the order of the division, or to set it aside, in whole or in part, or it may remand the proceeding to the division for such further action as it may direct. On such review, the findings and order of the division shall be conclusive on the parties, except that the order of the division may be set aside, in whole or in part, or remanded to the division, for failure of the division to comply with the requirements of this chapter, for failure of the order to conform, or confine itself, to matters within the scope of the division's jurisdiction, or for fraud or corruption by a member of the division making the order. The judgment of the court shall be subject to review as provided in sections 1291 and 1254 of title 28, United States Code.

(r) All actions at law based upon the provisions of this section shall be begun within two years from the time the cause of action accrues under the award of the division of the Adjustment Board, and not after....

Second. Nothing in this section shall be construed to prevent any individual carrier, system, or group of carriers and any class or classes of its or their employees, all acting through their representatives, selected in accordance with the provisions of this Act, from mutually agreeing to the establishment of system, group, or regional boards of adjustment for the purpose of adjusting and deciding disputes of the character specified in this section. In the event that either party to such a system, group, or regional board of adjustment is dissatisfied with such arrangement, it may upon ninety days' notice to the other party elect to come under the jurisdiction of the Adjustment Board....

NATIONAL MEDIATION BOARD

§ 4. First. The Board of Mediation is hereby abolished, effective thirty days from the date of approval of this Act and the members, secretary, officers, assistants, employees, and agents thereof, in office upon the date of approval of this Act, shall continue to function and receive their salaries for a period of thirty days from such date in the same manner as though this Act had not been passed. There is established, as an independent agency in the executive branch of the Government, a board to be known as the "National Mediation Board," to be composed of three members appointed by the President, by and with the advice and consent of the Senate, not more than two of whom shall be of the same political party. Each member of the Mediation Board in office on January 1, 1965, shall be deemed to have been appointed for a term of office which shall expire on July 1 of the year his term would have otherwise expired. The terms of office of all successors shall expire three years after the expiration of the terms for which their predecessors were appointed; but any member appointed to fill a vacancy occurring prior to the expiration of the term for which his predecessor was appointed shall be appointed only for the unexpired term of his predecessor. Vacancies in the Board shall not impair the powers nor affect the duties of the Board nor of the remaining members of the Board. Two of the members in office shall constitute a quorum for the transaction of the business of the Board....

A member of the Board may be removed by the President for inefficiency, neglect of duty, malfeasance in office, or ineligibility, but for no other cause. . . .

FUNCTIONS OF MEDIATION BOARD

§ 5. First. The parties, or either party, to a dispute between an employee or group of employees and a carrier may invoke the services of the Mediation Board in any of the following cases:

(a) A dispute concerning changes in rates of pay, rules, or working conditions not adjusted by the parties in conference.

(b) Any other dispute not referable to the National Railroad Adjustment Board and not adjusted in conference between the parties or where conferences are refused.

The Mediation Board may proffer its services in case any labor emergency is found by it to exist at any time.

In either event the said Board shall promptly put itself in communication with the parties to such controversy, and shall use its best efforts, by mediation, to bring them to agreement. If such efforts to bring about an amicable settlement through mediation shall be unsuccessful, the said Board shall at once endeavor as its final required action (except as provided in paragraph third of this section and in section 10 of this Act) to induce the parties to submit their controversy to arbitration, in accordance with the provisions of this Act.

If arbitration at the request of the Board shall be refused by one or both parties, the Board shall at once notify both parties in writing that its mediatory efforts have failed and for thirty days thereafter, unless in the intervening period the parties agree to arbitration, or an emergency board shall be created under section 10 of this Act, no change shall be made in the rates of pay, rules, or working conditions or establish practices in effect prior to the time the dispute arose.

Second. In any case in which a controversy arises over the meaning or the application of any agreement reached through mediation under the provisions of this Act, either party to the said agreement, or both, may apply to the Mediation Board for an interpretation of the meaning or application of such agreement. The said Board shall upon receipt of such request notify the parties to the controversy, and after a hearing of both sides give its interpretation within thirty days. . . .

PROCEDURE IN CHANGING RATES OF PAY, RULES, AND WORKING CONDITIONS

§ 6. Carriers and representatives of the employees shall give at least thirty days' written notice of an intended change in agreements affecting rates of pay, rules, or working conditions, and the time and place for the beginning of conference between the representatives of the parties interested in such intended changes shall be agreed upon within ten days after the receipt of said notice, and said time shall be within the thirty days provided in the notice. In every case where such notice of intended change has been given, or conferences are being held with reference thereto, or the services of the Mediation Board have been requested by either party, or said Board has proffered its services, rates of pay, rules, or working conditions shall not be altered by the carrier until the controversy has been finally acted upon, as required by section 5 of this Act, by the Mediation Board, unless a period of ten days has elapsed after termination of conferences without request for or proffer of the services of the Mediation Board.

ARBITRATION

§ 7. First. Whenever a controversy shall arise between a carrier or carriers and its or their employees which is not settled either in conference between representatives of the parties or by the appropriate adjustment board or through mediation in the manner provided in the preceding sections such controversy may, by agreement of the parties to such controversy, be submitted to the arbitration of a board of three (or, if the parties to the controversy so stipulate, of six) persons: *Provided, however,* That the failure or refusal of either party to submit a controversy to arbitration shall not be construed as a violation of any legal obligation imposed upon such party by the terms of this Act or otherwise.

Second. Such board of arbitration shall be chosen in the following manner:

(a) In the case of a board of three the carrier or carriers and the representatives of the employees, parties respectively to the agreement to arbitrate, shall each name one arbitrator; the two arbitrators thus chosen shall select a third arbitrator. If the arbitrators chosen by the parties shall fail to name the third arbitrator within five days after their first meeting, such third arbitrator shall be named by the Mediation Board.

(b) In the case of a board of six the carrier or carriers and the representatives of the employees, parties respectively to the agreement to arbitrate, shall each name two arbitrators; the four arbitrators thus chosen shall, by a majority vote, select the remaining two arbitrators. If the arbitrators chosen by the parties shall fail to name the two arbitrators within fifteen days after their first meeting, the said two arbitrators, or as many of them as have not been named, shall be named by the Mediation Board.

Third. (a) When the arbitrators selected by the respective parties have agreed upon the remaining arbitrator or arbitrators, they shall notify the Mediation Board, and, in the event of their failure to agree upon any or upon all of the necessary arbitrators within the period fixed by this Act, they shall, at the expiration of such period, notify the Mediation Board of the arbitrators selected, if any, or of their failure to make or complete such selection.

(b) The board of arbitration shall organize and select its own chairman and make all necessary rules for conducting its hearings: *Provided, however,* That the board of arbitration shall be bound to give the parties to the controversy a full and fair hearing, which shall include an opportunity to present evidence in support of their claims, and an opportunity to present their case in person, by counsel, or by other representative as they may respectively elect....

§ **9. First.** The award of a board of arbitration, having been acknowledged as herein provided, shall be filed in the clerk's office of the district court designated in the agreement to arbitrate.

Second. An award acknowledged and filed as herein provided shall be conclusive on the parties as to the merits and facts of the controversy submitted to arbitration, and unless, within ten days after the filing of the award, a petition to impeach the award, on the grounds hereinafter set forth, shall be filed in the clerk's office of the court in which the award has been filed, the court shall enter judgment on the award, which judgment shall be final and conclusive on the parties.

Third. Such petition for the impeachment or contesting of any award so filed shall be entertained by the court only on one or more of the following grounds:

(a) That the award plainly does not conform to the substantive requirements laid down by this Act for such awards, or that the proceedings were not substantially in conformity with this Act;

(b) That the award does not conform, nor confine itself, to the stipulations of the agreement to arbitrate; or

(c) That a member of the board of arbitration rendering the award was guilty of fraud or corruption; or that a party to the arbitration practiced fraud or corruption which fraud or corruption affected the result of the arbitration: *Provided, however,* That no court shall entertain any such petition on the ground that an award is invalid for uncertainty; in such case the proper remedy shall be a submission of such award to a reconvened board, or subcommittee thereof, for interpretation, as provided by this Act: *Provided further,* That an award contested as herein provided shall be construed liberally by the court, with a view to favoring its validity, and that no award shall be set aside for trivial irregularity or clerical error, going only to form and not to substance....

Eighth. Nothing in this Act shall be construed to require an individual employee to render labor or service without his consent, nor shall anything in this Act be construed to make the quitting of his labor or service by an individual employee an illegal act; nor shall any court issue any process to compel the performance by an individual employee of such labor or service, without his consent.

EMERGENCY BOARD

§ 10. If a dispute between a carrier and its employees be not adjusted under the foregoing provisions of this Act and should, in the judgment of the Mediation Board, threaten substantially to interrupt interstate commerce to a degree such as to deprive any section of the country of essential transportation service, the Mediation Board shall notify the President, who may thereupon, in his discretion, create a board to investigate and report respecting such dispute. Such board shall be composed of such number of persons as to the President may seem desirable: *Provided, however,* That no member appointed shall be pecuniarily or otherwise interested in any organization of employees or any carrier. The compensation of the members of any such board shall be fixed by the President. Such board shall be created separately in each instance and it shall investigate promptly the facts as to the dispute and make a report thereon to the President within thirty days from the date of its creation. . . .

After the creation of such board and for thirty days after such board has made its report to the President, no change, except by agreement, shall be made by the parties to the controversy in the conditions out of which the dispute arose. . . .

TITLE II

§ 201. All of the provisions of title I of this Act, except the provisions of section 3 thereof, are extended to and shall cover every common carrier by air engaged in interstate or foreign commerce, and every carrier by air transporting mail for or under contract with the United States Government, and every air pilot or other person who performs any work as an employee or subordinate official of such carrier or carriers, subject to its or their continuing authority to supervise and direct the manner of rendition of his service.

§ 202. The duties, requirements, penalties, benefits, and privileges prescribed and established by the provisions of title I of this Act, except section 3 thereof, shall apply to said carriers by air and their employees in the same manner and to the same extent as though such carriers and their employees were specifically included within the definition of "carrier" and "employee", respectively, in section 1 thereof.

§ 203. The parties or either party to a dispute between an employee or a group of employees and a carrier or carriers by air may invoke the services of the National Mediation Board and the jurisdiction of said Mediation Board is extended to any of the following cases:

(a) A dispute concerning changes in rates of pay, rules, or working conditions not adjusted by the parties in conference.

(b) Any other dispute not referable to an adjustment board, as hereinafter provided, and not adjusted in conference between the parties, or where conferences are refused.

The National Mediation Board may proffer its services in case any labor emergency is found by it to exist at any time.

The services of the Mediation Board may be invoked in a case under this title in the same manner and to the same extent as are the disputes covered by section 5 of title I of this Act.

§ 204. The disputes between an employee or group of employees and a carrier or carriers by air growing out of grievances, or out of interpretation or application of agreements concerning rates of pay, rules, or working conditions, including cases pending and unadjusted on aPRIL 10, 1936 before the National Labor Relations Board, shall be handled in the usual manner up to and including the chief operating officer of the carrier designated to handle such disputes; but, failing to reach an adjustment in this manner, the disputes may be referred by petition of the parties or by either party to an appropriate adjustment board, as hereinafter provided, with a full statement of the facts and supporting data bearing upon the disputes.

It shall be the duty of every carrier and of its employees, acting through their representatives, selected in accordance with the provisions of this title, to establish a board of adjustment of jurisdiction not exceeding the jurisdiction which may be lawfully exercised by system, group, or regional boards of adjustment, under the authority of section 3, title I, of this Act.

Such boards of adjustment may be established by agreement between employees and carriers either on any individual carrier, or system, or group of carriers by air and any class or classes of its or their employees; or pending the establishment of a permanent National Board of Adjustment as hereinafter provided. Nothing in this Act shall prevent said carriers by air, or any class or classes of their employees, both acting through their representatives selected in accordance with provisions of this title from mutually agreeing to the establishment of a National Board of Adjustment of temporary duration and of similarly limited jurisdiction....

§ 207. If any provision of this title or application thereof to any person or circumstance is held invalid, the remainder of the Act and the application of such provision to other persons or circumstances shall not be affected thereby....

LABOR MANAGEMENT RELATIONS ACT

Pub. L. No. 101, 80th Cong., 1st Sess. (1947), 61 Stat. 136, as amended by
Pub. L. No. 257, 86th Cong., 1st Sess. (1959), 73 Stat. 541; and Pub. L.
No. 93-360, 93d Cong., 2d Sess. (1974), 88 Stat. 395; 29 U.S.C. §§ 141
et seq.

SHORT TITLE AND DECLARATION OF POLICY

§ 1. (a) This Act may be cited as the "Labor Management Relations
Act, 1947."

(b) Industrial strife which interferes with the normal flow of commerce
and with the full production of articles and commodities for commerce, can
be avoided or substantially minimized if employers, employees, and labor
organizations each recognize under law one another's legitimate rights in
their relations with each other, and above all recognize under law that
neither party has any right in its relations with any other to engage in acts
or practices which jeopardize the public health, safety, or interest.

It is the purpose and policy of this Act, in order to promote the full
flow of commerce, to prescribe the legitimate rights of both employees and
employers in their relations affecting commerce, to provide orderly and
peaceful procedures for preventing the interference by either with the
legitimate rights of the other, to protect the rights of individual employees
in their relations with labor organizations whose activities affect commerce,
to define and proscribe practices on the part of labor and management
which affect commerce and are inimical to the general welfare, and to
protect the rights of the public in connection with labor disputes affecting
commerce.

TITLE I. AMENDMENT OF NATIONAL LABOR RELATIONS ACT [49 Stat. 449 (1935)]

§ 101. The National Labor Relations Act is hereby amended to read as
follows:*

FINDINGS AND POLICIES

§ 1. The denial by **some** employers of the right of employees to
organize and the refusal by **some** employers to accept the procedure of
collective bargaining lead to strikes and other forms of industrial strife or
unrest, which have the intent or the necessary effect of burdening or
obstructing commerce by (a) impairing the efficiency, safety, or operation of
the instrumentalities of commerce; (b) occurring in the current of commerce; (c) materially affecting, restraining, or controlling the flow of raw

---

* The text of the original NLRA (Wagner
Act) is in roman type. Provisions added by
the LMRA in 1947 (Taft-Hartley Act) are in
boldface type; further amendments made by
the LMRDA of 1959 (Landrum-Griffin Act)
are in italics; and provisions added by the
Health Care Institutions Act of 1974 are capi-
talized. Material deleted by any of these
amendments is enclosed in brackets.—ED.

materials or manufactured or processed goods from or into the channels of commerce, or the prices of such materials or goods in commerce; or (d) causing diminution of employment and wages in such volume as substantially to impair or disrupt the market for goods flowing from or into the channels of commerce.

The inequality of bargaining power between employees who do not possess full freedom of association or actual liberty of contract, and employers who are organized in the corporate or other forms of ownership association substantially burdens and affects the flow of commerce, and tends to aggravate recurrent business depressions, by depressing wage rates and the purchasing power of wage earners in industry and by preventing the stabilization of competitive wage rates and working conditions within and between industries.

Experience has proved that protection by law of the right of employees to organize and bargain collectively safeguards commerce from injury, impairment, or interruption, and promotes the flow of commerce by removing certain recognized sources of industrial strife and unrest, by encouraging practices fundamental to the friendly adjustment of industrial disputes arising out of differences as to wages, hour, or other working conditions, and by restoring equality of bargaining power between employers and employees.

Experience has further demonstrated that certain practices by some labor organizations, their officers, and members have the intent or the necessary effect of burdening or obstructing commerce by preventing the free flow of goods in such commerce through strikes and other forms of industrial unrest or through concerted activities which impair the interest of the public in the free flow of such commerce. The elimination of such practices is a necessary condition to the assurance of the rights herein guaranteed.

It is hereby declared to be the policy of the United States to eliminate the causes of certain substantial obstructions to the free flow of commerce and to mitigate and eliminate these obstructions when they have occurred by encouraging the practice and procedure of collective bargaining and by protecting the exercise by workers of full freedom of association, self-organization, and designation of representatives of their own choosing, for the purpose of negotiating the terms and conditions of their employment or other mutual aid or protection.

DEFINITIONS

§ 2.   When used in this Act—

(1) The term "person" includes one or more individuals, labor organizations, partnerships, associations, corporations, legal representatives, trustees, trustees in bankruptcy, or receivers.

(2) The term "employer" includes any person acting [in the interest] **as an agent** of an employer, directly or indirectly, but shall not include the United States **or any wholly owned Government corporation, or any Federal Reserve Bank,** or any State or political subdivision thereof, [**or any corporation or association operating a hospital, if no part of the net earnings inures to the benefit of any private shareholder or individual,**] or any person subject to the Railway Labor Act, as amended from time to time, or any labor organization (other than when acting as an employer), or anyone acting in the capacity of officer or agent of such labor organization.

(3) The term "employee" shall include any employee, and shall not be limited to the employees of a particular employer, unless the Act explicitly states otherwise, and shall include any individual whose work has ceased as a consequence of, or in connection with, any current labor dispute or because of any unfair labor practice, and who has not obtained any other regular and substantially equivalent employment, but shall not include any individual employed as an agricultural laborer, or in the domestic service of any family or person at his home, or any individual employed by his parent or spouse, **or any individual having the status of an independent contractor, or any individual employed as a supervisor, or any individual employed by an employer subject to the Railway Labor Act, as amended from time to time, or by any other person who is not an employer as herein defined.**

— Southern chairs exacting racial tint to the statute.

(4) The term "representatives" includes any individual or labor organization.

(5) The term "labor organization" means any organization of any kind, or any agency or employee representation committee or plan, in which employees participate and which exists for the purpose, in whole or in part, of dealing with employers concerning grievances, labor disputes, wages, rates of pay, hours of employment, or conditions of work.

(6) The term "commerce" means trade, traffic, commerce, transportation, or communication among the several States, or between the District of Columbia or any Territory of the United States and any State or other Territory, or between any foreign country and any State, Territory, or the District of Columbia, or within the District of Columbia or any Territory, or between points in the same State but through any other State or any Territory or the District of Columbia or any foreign country.

(7) The term "affecting commerce" means in commerce, or burdening or obstructing commerce or the free flow of commerce, or having led or tending to lead to a labor dispute burdening or obstructing commerce or the free flow of commerce.

(8) The term "unfair labor practice" means any unfair labor practice listed in section 8.

(9) The term "labor dispute" includes any controversy concerning terms, tenure or conditions of employment, or concerning the association or representation of persons in negotiating, fixing, maintaining, changing, or seeking to arrange terms or conditions of employment, regardless of whether the disputants stand in the proximate relation of employer and employee.

(10) The term "National Labor Relations Board" means the National Labor Relations Board provided for in section 3 of this Act.

(11) The term "supervisor" means any individual having authority, in the interest of the employer, to hire, transfer, suspend, lay off, recall, promote, discharge, assign, reward, or discipline other employees, or responsibly to direct them, or to adjust their grievances, or effectively to recommend such action, if in connection with the foregoing the exercise of such authority is not of a merely routine or clerical nature, but requires the use of independent judgment.

(12) The term "professional employee" means—

(a) any employee engaged in work (i) predominantly intellectual and varied in character as opposed to routine mental, manual, mechanical, or physical work; (ii) involving the consistent exercise of discretion and judgment in its performance; (iii) of such a character that the output produced or the result accomplished cannot be standardized in relation to a given period of time; (iv) requiring knowledge of an advanced type in a field of science or learning customarily acquired by a prolonged course of specialized intellectual instruction and study in an institution of higher learning or a hospital, as distinguished from a general academic education or from an apprenticeship or from training in the performance of routine mental, manual, or physical processes; or

(b) any employee, who (i) has completed the courses of specialized intellectual instruction and study described in clause (iv) of paragraph (a), and (ii) is performing related work under the supervision of a professional person to qualify himself to become a professional employee as defined in paragraph (a).

(13) In determining whether any person is acting as an "agent" of another person so as to make such other person responsible for his acts, the question of whether the specific acts performed were actually authorized or subsequently ratified shall not be controlling.

(14) THE TERM "HEALTH CARE INSTITUTION" SHALL IN-
CLUDE ANY HOSPITAL, CONVALESCENT HOSPITAL, HEALTH
MAINTENANCE ORGANIZATION, HEALTH CLINIC, NURSING
HOME, EXTENDED CARE FACILITY, OR OTHER INSTITUTION DE-
VOTED TO THE CARE OF SICK, INFIRM, OR AGED PERSON.

NATIONAL LABOR RELATIONS BOARD

§ 3. (a) The National Labor Relations Board (hereinafter
called the "Board") created by this Act prior to its amendment by
the Labor Management Relations Act, 1947, is hereby continued as
an agency of the United States, except that the Board shall consist
of five instead of three members, appointed by the President by
and with the advice and consent of the Senate. Of the two
additional members so provided for, one shall be appointed for a
term of five years and the other for a term of two years. Their
successors, and the successors of the other members, shall be
appointed for terms of five years each, excepting that any individual chosen to fill a vacancy shall be appointed only for the unexpired term of the member whom he shall succeed. The President
shall designate one member to serve as Chairman of the Board.
Any member of the Board may be removed by the President, upon
notice and hearing, for neglect of duty or malfeasance in office,
but for no other cause.

(b) The Board is authorized to delegate to any group of three
or more members any or all of the powers which it may itself
exercise. *The Board is also authorized to delegate to its regional directors
its powers under section 9 to determine the unit appropriate for the purpose
of collective bargaining, to investigate and provide for hearings, and determine whether a question of representation exists, and to direct an election or
take a secret ballot under subsection (c) or (e) of section 9 and certify the
results thereof, except that upon the filing of a request therefor with the
Board by any interested person, the Board may review any action of a
regional director delegated to him under this paragraph, but such a review
shall not, unless specifically ordered by the Board, operate as a stay of any
action taken by the regional director.* A vacancy in the Board shall not
impair the right of the remaining members to exercise all of the
powers of the Board, and three members of the Board shall, at all
times, constitute a quorum of the Board, except that two members
shall constitute a quorum of any group designated pursuant to the
first sentence hereof. The Board shall have an official seal which
shall be judicially noticed....

(d) There shall be a General Counsel of the Board who shall be
appointed by the President, by and with the advice and consent of
the Senate, for a term of four years. The General Counsel of the
Board shall exercise general supervision over all attorneys employed by the Board (other than trial examiners and legal assis-

tants to Board members) and over the officers and employees in the regional offices. He shall have final authority, on behalf of the Board, in respect of the investigation of charges and issuance of complaints under section 10, and in respect of the prosecution of such complaints before the Board, and shall have such other duties as the Board may prescribe or as may be provided by law. *In case of a vacancy in the office of the General Counsel the President is authorized to designate the officer or employee who shall act as General Counsel during such vacancy, but no person or persons so designated shall so act (1) for more than forty days when the Congress is in session unless a nomination to fill such vacancy shall have been submitted to the Senate, or (2) after the adjournment sine die of the session of the Senate in which such nomination was submitted.*

§ 4. (a) Each member of the Board and the General Counsel of the Board shall ... be eligible for reappointment, and shall not engage in any other business, vocation, or employment. The Board shall appoint an executive secretary, and such attorneys, examiners, and regional directors, and such other employees as it may from time to time find necessary for the proper performance of its duties. The Board may not employ any attorneys for the purpose of reviewing transcripts of hearings or preparing drafts of opinions except that any attorney employed for assignment as a legal assistant to any Board member may for such Board member review such transcripts and prepare such drafts. No trial examiner's report shall be reviewed, either before or after its publication, by any person other than a member of the Board or his legal assistant, and no trial examiner shall advise or consult with the Board with respect to exceptions taken to his findings, rulings, or recommendations. The Board may establish or utilize such regional, local, or other agencies, and utilize such voluntary and uncompensated services, as may from time to time be needed. Attorneys appointed under this section may, at the direction of the Board, appear for and represent the Board in any case in court. Nothing in this Act shall be construed to authorize the Board to appoint individuals for the purpose of conciliation or mediation, or for economic analysis....

§ 5. The principal office of the Board shall be in the District of Columbia, but it may meet and exercise any or all of its powers at any other place. The Board may, by one or more of its members or by such agents or agencies as it may designate, prosecute any inquiry necessary to its functions in any part of the United States. A member who participates in such an inquiry shall not be disqualified from subsequently participating in a decision of the Board in the same case.

§ 6. The Board shall have authority from time to time to make, amend, and rescind, **in the manner prescribed by the Administrative**

Procedure Act, such rules and regulations as may be necessary to carry out the provisions of this Act.

RIGHT OF EMPLOYEES

§ 7. Employees shall have the right to self-organization, to form, join, or assist labor organizations, to bargain collectively through representatives of their own choosing, and to engage in **other** concerted activities for the purpose of collective bargaining or other mutual aid or protection, **and shall also have the right to refrain from any or all of such activities except to the extent that such right may be affected by an agreement requiring membership in a labor organization as a condition of employment as authorized in section 8(a)(3).**

UNFAIR LABOR PRACTICES

§ 8(a). It shall be an unfair labor practice for an employer—

(1) to interfere with, restrain, or coerce employees in the exercise of the rights guaranteed in section 7;

(2) to dominate or interfere with the formation or administration of any labor organization or contribute financial or other support to it: *Provided*, That subject to rules and regulations made and published by the Board pursuant to section 6, an employer shall not be prohibited from permitting employees to confer with him during working hours without loss of time or pay;

(3) by discrimination in regard to hire or tenure of employment or any term or condition of employment to encourage or discourage membership in any labor organization: *Provided*, That nothing in this Act, or in any other statute of the United States, shall preclude an employer from making an agreement with a labor organization (not established, maintained, or assisted by any action defined in section 8(a) of this Act as an unfair labor practice) to require as a condition of employment membership therein **on or after the thirtieth day following the beginning of such employment or the effective date of such agreement, whichever is the later,** (i) if such labor organization is the representative of the employees as provided in section 9(a), in the appropriate collective-bargaining unit covered by such agreement when made, **[and has at the time the agreement was made or within the preceding twelve months received from the Board a notice of compliance with section 9(f), (g), (h)], and (ii) unless following an election held as provided in section 9(e) within one year preceding the effective date of such agreement, the Board shall have certified that at least a majority of the employees eligible to vote in such election have voted to rescind the authority of such labor organization to make such an agreement: *Provided further*, That no employer shall justify any discrimination against an employee for nonmembership in a labor organization (A) if he has reasonable grounds for believing that such membership was not available to the employee on the same**

terms and conditions generally applicable to other members, or (B) if he has reasonable grounds for believing that membership was denied or terminated for reasons other than the failure of the employee to tender the periodic dues and the initiation fees uniformly required as a condition of acquiring or retaining membership;

(4) to discharge or otherwise discriminate against an employee because he has filed charges or given testimony under this Act;

(5) to refuse to bargain collectively with the representatives of his employees, subject to the provisions of section 9(a).

(b) It shall be an unfair labor practice for a labor organization or its agents—

(1) to restrain or coerce (A) employees in the exercise of the rights guaranteed in section 7: *Provided,* **That this paragraph shall not impair the right of a labor organization to prescribe its own rules with respect to the acquisition or retention of membership therein; or (B) an employer in the selection of his representatives for the purposes of collective bargaining or the adjustment of grievances;**

(2) to cause or attempt to cause an employer to discriminate against an employee in violation of subsection (a)(3) or to discriminate against an employee with respect to whom membership in such organization has been denied or terminated on some ground other than his failure to tender the periodic dues and the initiation fees uniformly required as a condition of acquiring or retaining membership;

(3) to refuse to bargain collectively with an employer, provided it is the representative of his employees subject to the provisions of section 9(a);

(4)(i) to engage in, or to induce or encourage [the employees of any employer] *any individual employed by any person engaged in commerce or in an industry affecting commerce* **to engage in, a strike or a [concerted] refusal in the course of [their]** *his* **employment to use, manufacture, process, transport, or otherwise handle or work on any goods, articles, materials, or commodities or to perform any services[,];** *or (ii) to threaten, coerce, or restrain any person engaged in commerce or in an industry affecting commerce,* **where** *in either case* **an object thereof is:**

(A) forcing or requiring any employer or self-employed person to join any labor or employer organization or [any employer or other person to cease using, selling, handling, transporting, or otherwise dealing in the products of any other producer, processor, or manufacturer, or to cease doing

business with any other person] *to enter into any agreement which is prohibited by section (e)*;

(B) *forcing or requiring any person to cease using, selling, handling, transporting, or otherwise dealing in the products of any other producer, processor, or manufacturer, or to cease doing business with any other person, or* **forcing or requiring any other employer to recognize or bargain with a labor organization as the representative of his employees unless such labor organization has been certified as the representative of such employees under the provisions of section 9**[;]: *Provided, That nothing contained in this clause (B) shall be construed to make unlawful, where not otherwise unlawful, any primary strike or primary picketing*;

(C) forcing or requiring any employer to recognize or bargain with a particular labor organization as the representative of his employees if another labor organization has been certified as the representative of such employees under the provisions of section 9;

(D) forcing or requiring any employer to assign particular work to employees in a particular labor organization or in a particular trade, craft, or class rather than to employees in another labor organization or in another trade, craft, or class, unless such employer is failing to conform to an order or certification of the Board determining the bargaining representative for employees performing such work:

Provided, **That nothing contained in this subsection (b) shall be construed to make unlawful a refusal by any person to enter upon the premises of any employer (other than his own employer), if the employees of such employer are engaged in a strike ratified or approved by a representative of such employees whom such employer is required to recognize under this Act**[;]: *Provided further, That for the purposes of this paragraph (4) only, nothing contained in such paragraph shall be construed to prohibit publicity, other than picketing, for the purpose of truthfully advising the public, including consumers and members of a labor organization, that a product or products are produced by an employer with whom the labor organization has a primary dispute and are distributed by another employer, as long as such publicity does not have an effect of inducing any individual employed by any person other than the primary employer in the course of his employment to refuse to pick up, deliver, or transport any goods, or not to perform any services, at the establishment of the employer engaged in such distribution;*

(5) to require of employees covered by an agreement authorized under subsection (a)(3) the payment, as a condition precedent to becoming a member of such organization, of a fee in an amount

which the Board finds excessive or discriminatory under all the circumstances. In making such a finding, the Board shall consider, among other relevant factors, the practices and customs of labor organizations in the particular industry, and the wages currently paid to the employees affected; [and]

(6) to cause or attempt to cause an employer to pay or deliver or agree to pay or deliver any money or other thing of value, in the nature of an exaction, for services which are not performed or not to be performed[.]; *and*

(7) to picket or cause to be picketed, or threaten to picket or cause to be picketed, any employer where an object thereof is forcing or requiring an employer to recognize or bargain with a labor organization as the representative of his employees, or forcing or requiring the employees of an employer to accept or select such labor organization as their collective bargaining representative, unless such labor organization is currently certified as the representative of such employees:

(A) where the employer has lawfully recognized in accordance with this Act any other labor organization and a question concerning representation may not appropriately be raised under section 9(c) of this Act,

(B) where within the preceding twelve months a valid election under section 9(c) of this Act has been conducted, or

(C) where such picketing has been conducted without a petition under section 9(c) being filed within a reasonable period of time not to exceed thirty days from the commencement of such picketing: **Provided**, *That when such a petition has been filed the Board shall forthwith, without regard to the provisions of section 9(c)(1) or the absence of a showing of a substantial interest on the part of the labor organization, direct an election in such unit as the Board finds to be appropriate and shall certify the results thereof:* **Provided further**, *That nothing in this subparagraph (C) shall be construed to prohibit any picketing or other publicity for the purpose of truthfully advising the public (including consumers) that an employer does not employ members of, or have a contract with, a labor organization, unless an effect of such picketing is to induce any individual employed by any other person in the course of his employment, not to pick up, deliver or transport any goods or not to perform any services.*

Nothing in this paragraph (7) shall be construed to permit any act which would otherwise be an unfair labor practice under this section 8(b)..

(c) The expressing of any views, argument, or opinion, or the dissemination thereof, whether in written, printed, graphic, or visual form, shall not constitute or be evidence of an unfair labor practice under any of the provisions of this Act, if such expression contains no threat of reprisal or force or promise of benefit.

(d) For the purposes of this section, to bargain collectively is the performance of the mutual obligation of the employer and the representative of the employees to meet at reasonable times and confer in good faith with respect to wages, hours, and other terms and conditions of employment, or the negotiation of an agreement, or any question arising thereunder, and the execution of a written contract incorporating any agreement reached if requested by either party, but such obligation does not compel either party to agree to a proposal or require the making of a concession: *Provided*, That where there is in effect a collective-bargaining contract covering employees in an industry affecting commerce, the duty to bargain collectively shall also mean that no party to such contract shall terminate or modify such contract, unless the party desiring such termination or modification—

(1) serves a written notice upon the other party to the contract of the proposed termination or modification sixty days prior to the expiration date thereof, or in the event such contract contains no expiration date, sixty days prior to the time it is proposed to make such termination or modification;

(2) offers to meet and confer with the other party for the purpose of negotiating a new contract or a contract containing the proposed modifications;

(3) notifies the Federal Mediation and Conciliation Service within thirty days after such notice of the existence of a dispute, and simultaneously therewith notifies any State or Territorial agency established to mediate and conciliate disputes within the State or Territory where the dispute occurred, provided no agreement has been reached by that time; and

(4) continues in full force and effect, without resorting to strike or lockout, all the terms and conditions of the existing contract for a period of sixty days after such notice is given or until the expiration date of such contract, whichever occurs later;

The duties imposed upon employers, employees, and labor organizations by paragraphs (2), (3), and (4) shall become inapplicable upon an intervening certification of the Board, under which the labor organization or individual, which is a party to the contract, has been superseded as or ceased to be the representative of the employees subject to the provisions of section 9(a), and the duties so imposed shall not be construed as requiring either party to discuss or agree to any modification of the terms and conditions contained in a contract for a fixed period, if such modification is to become effective before such terms and conditions can be

reopened under the provisions of the contract. Any employee who engages in a strike within [the sixty-day] ANY NOTICE period specified in this subsection, OR WHO ENGAGES IN ANY STRIKE WITHIN THE APPROPRIATE PERIOD SPECIFIED IN SUBSECTION (g) OF THIS SECTION shall lose his status as an employee of the employer engaged in the particular labor dispute, for the purposes of sections 8, 9 and 10 of this Act, as amended, but such loss of status for such employee shall terminate if and when he is reemployed by such employer. WHENEVER THE COLLECTIVE BARGAINING INVOLVES EMPLOYEES OF A HEALTH CARE INSTITUTION, THE PROVISIONS OF THIS SUBSECTION SHALL BE MODIFIED AS FOLLOWS:

(A) THE NOTICE OF SECTION 8(d)(1) SHALL BE NINETY DAYS; THE NOTICE OF SECTION 8(d)(3) SHALL BE SIXTY DAYS; AND THE CONTRACT PERIOD OF SECTION 8(d)(4) SHALL BE NINETY DAYS.

(B) WHERE THE BARGAINING IS FOR AN INITIAL AGREEMENT FOLLOWING CERTIFICATION OR RECOGNITION, AT LEAST THIRTY DAYS' NOTICE OF THE EXISTENCE OF A DISPUTE SHALL BE GIVEN BY THE LABOR ORGANIZATION TO THE AGENCIES SET FORTH IN SECTION 8(d)(3).

(C) AFTER NOTICE IS GIVEN TO THE FEDERAL MEDIATION AND CONCILIATION SERVICE UNDER EITHER CLAUSE (A) OR (B) OF THIS SENTENCE, THE SERVICE SHALL PROMPTLY COMMUNICATE WITH THE PARTIES AND USE ITS BEST EFFORTS, BY MEDIATION AND CONCILIATION, TO BRING THEM TO AGREEMENT. THE PARTIES SHALL PARTICIPATE FULLY AND PROMPTLY IN SUCH MEETINGS AS MAY BE UNDERTAKEN BY THE SERVICE FOR THE PURPOSE OF AIDING IN A SETTLEMENT OF THE DISPUTE.

(e) It shall be an unfair labor practice for any labor organization and any employer to enter into any contract or agreement, express or implied, whereby such employer ceases or refrains or agrees to cease or refrain from handling, using, selling, transporting or otherwise dealing in any of the products of any other employer, or to cease doing business with any other person, and any contract or agreement entered into heretofore or hereafter containing such an agreement shall be to such extent unenforceable and void: Provided, *That nothing in this subsection (e) shall apply to an agreement between a labor organization and an employer in the construction industry relating to the contracting or subcontracting of work to be done at the site of the construction, alteration, painting, or repair of a building, structure, or other work:* Provided further, *That for the purposes of this subsection (e) and section 8(b)(4)(B) the terms "any employer", "any person engaged in commerce or an industry affecting commerce", and "any person" when used in relation to the terms "any other producer, processor, or*

manufacturer", "any other employer", or "any other person" shall not include persons in the relation of a jobber, manufacturer, contractor, or subcontractor working on the goods or premises of the jobber or manufacturer or performing parts of an integrated process of production in the apparel and clothing industry: Provided further, *That nothing in this Act shall prohibit the enforcement of any agreement which is within the foregoing exception.*

(f) It shall not be an unfair labor practice under subsections (a) and (b) of this section for an employer engaged primarily in the building and construction industry to make an agreement covering employees engaged (or who, upon their employment, will be engaged) in the building and construction industry with a labor organization of which building and construction employees are members (not established, maintained, or assisted by any action defined in section 8(a) of this Act as an unfair labor practice) because (1) the majority status of such labor organization has not been established under the provisions of section 9 of this Act prior to the making of such agreement, or (2) such agreement requires as a condition of employment, membership in such labor organization after the seventh day following the beginning of such employment or the effective date of the agreement, whichever is later, or (3) such agreement requires the employer to notify such labor organization of opportunities for employment with such employer, or gives such labor organization an opportunity to refer qualified applicants for such employment, or (4) such agreement specifies minimum training or experience qualifications for employment or provides for priority in opportunities for employment based upon length of service with such employer, in the industry or in the particular geographical area: Provided, *That nothing in this subsection shall set aside the final proviso to section 8(a)(3) of this Act:* Provided further, *That any agreement which would be invalid, but for clause (1) of this subsection, shall not be a bar to a petition filed pursuant to section 9(c) or 9(e).* *

(G) A LABOR ORGANIZATION BEFORE ENGAGING IN ANY STRIKE, PICKETING, OR OTHER CONCERTED REFUSAL TO WORK AT ANY HEALTH CARE INSTITUTION SHALL, NOT LESS THAN TEN DAYS PRIOR TO SUCH ACTION, NOTIFY THE INSTITUTION IN WRITING AND THE FEDERAL MEDIATION AND CONCILIATION SERVICE OF THAT INTENTION, EXCEPT THAT IN THE CASE OF BARGAINING FOR AN INITIAL AGREEMENT FOLLOWING CERTIFICATION OR RECOGNITION THE NOTICE REQUIRED BY THIS SUBSEC-

* Section 8(f) is inserted in the Act by subsection (a) of Section 705 of Public Law 86-257. Section 705(b) provides: "Nothing contained in the amendment made by subsection (a) shall be construed as authorizing the execution or application of agreements requiring membership in a labor organization as a condition of employment in any State or Territory in which such execution or application is prohibited by State or Territorial law."—Ed.

TION SHALL NOT BE GIVEN UNTIL THE EXPIRATION OF THE PERIOD SPECIFIED IN CLAUSE (B) OF THE LAST SENTENCE OF SECTION 8(d) OF THIS Act. THE NOTICE SHALL STATE THE DATE AND TIME THAT SUCH ACTION WILL COMMENCE. THE NOTICE, ONCE GIVEN, MAY BE EXTENDED BY THE WRITTEN AGREEMENT OF BOTH PARTIES.

REPRESENTATIVES AND ELECTIONS

§ 9. (a) Representatives designated or selected for the purposes of collective bargaining by the majority of the employees in a unit appropriate for such purposes, shall be the exclusive representatives of all the employees in such unit for the purposes of collective bargaining in respect to rates of pay, wages, hours of employment, or other conditions of employment: *Provided*, That any individual employee or a group of employees shall have the right at any time to present grievances to their employer **and to have such grievances adjusted, without the intervention of the bargaining representative, as long as the adjustment is not inconsistent with the terms of a collective-bargaining contract or agreement then in effect: *Provided further*, That the bargaining representative has been given opportunity to be present at such adjustment.**

(b) The Board shall decide in each case whether, in order to assure to employees the fullest freedom in exercising the rights guaranteed by this Act, the unit appropriate for the purposes of collective bargaining shall be the employer unit, craft unit, plant unit, or subdivision thereof: ***Provided*, That the Board shall not (1) decide that any unit is appropriate for such purposes if such unit includes both professional employees and employees who are not professional employees unless a majority of such professional employees vote for inclusion in such unit; or (2) decide that any craft unit is inappropriate for such purposes on the ground that a different unit has been established by a prior Board determination, unless a majority of the employees in the proposed craft unit vote against separate representation or (3) decide that any unit is appropriate for such purposes if it includes, together with other employees, any individual employed as a guard to enforce against employees and other persons rules to protect property of the employer or to protect the safety of persons on the employer's premises; but no labor organization shall be certified as the representative of employees in a bargaining unit of guards if such organization admits to membership, or is affiliated directly or indirectly with an organization which admits to membership, employees other than guards.**

[(c) Whenever a question affecting commerce arises concerning the representation of employees, the Board may investigate such controversy and certify to the parties, in writing, the name or names of the representatives that have been designated or selected. In any such investigation, the Board shall provide for an appropriate hearing upon due notice, either in conjunction with a proceeding under section 10 or otherwise, and may take a secret ballot of employees, or utilize any other suitable method to ascertain such representatives.]

(c)(1) **Whenever a petition shall have been filed, in accordance with such regulations as may be prescribed by the Board—**

(A) **by an employee or group of employees or any individual or labor organization acting in their behalf alleging that a substantial number of employees (i) wish to be represented for collective bargaining and that their employer declines to recognize their representative as the representative defined in section 9(a), or (ii) assert that the individual or labor organization, which has been certified or is being currently recognized by their employer as the bargaining representative, is no longer a representative as defined in section 9(a); or**

(B) **by an employer, alleging that one or more individuals or labor organizations have presented to him a claim to be recognized as the representative defined in section 9(a);**

the Board shall investigate such petition and if it has reasonable cause to believe that a question of representation affecting commerce exists shall provide for an appropriate hearing upon due notice. Such hearing may be conducted by an officer or employee of the regional office, who shall not make any recommendations with respect thereto. If the Board finds upon the record of such hearing that such a question of representation exists, it shall direct an election by secret ballot and shall certify the results thereof.

(2) **In determining whether or not a question of representation affecting commerce exists, the same regulations and rules of decision shall apply irrespective of the identity of the persons filing the petition or the kind of relief sought and in no case shall the Board deny a labor organization a place on the ballot by reason of an order with respect to such labor organization or its predecessor not issued in conformity with section 10(c).**

(3) **No election shall be directed in any bargaining unit or any subdivision within which, in the preceding twelve-month period, a valid election shall have been held. Employees [on]** *engaged in an economic* **strike who are not entitled to reinstatement shall [not] be eligible to vote**[.] *under such regulations as the Board shall find are consistent with the purposes and provisions of this Act in any election conducted within twelve months after the commencement of the strike.* **In any election where none of the choices on the ballot receives a majority, a run-off shall be conducted, the ballot providing for a**

selection between the two choices receiving the largest and second largest number of valid votes cast in the election.

(4) Nothing in this section shall be construed to prohibit the waiving of hearings by stipulation for the purpose of a consent election in conformity with regulations and rules of decision of the Board.

(5) In determining whether a unit is appropriate for the purposes specified in subsection (b) the extent to which the employees have organized shall not be controlling.

(d) Whenever an order of the Board made pursuant to section 10(c) is based in whole or in part upon facts certified following an investigation pursuant to subsection (c) of this section and there is a petition for the enforcement or review of such order, such certification and the record of such investigation shall be included in the transcript of the entire record required to be filed under section 10(e) or 10(f), and thereupon the decree of the court enforcing, modifying, or setting aside in whole or in part the order of the Board shall be made and entered upon the pleadings, testimony, and proceedings set forth in such transcript.

[(e)(1) Upon the filing with the Board by a labor organization, which is the representative of employees as provided in section 9(a), of a petition alleging that 30 per centum or more of the employees within a unit claimed to be appropriate for such purposes desire to authorize such labor organization to make an agreement with the employer of such employees requiring membership in such labor organization as a condition of employment in such unit, upon an appropriate showing thereof the Board shall, if no question of representation exists, take a secret ballot of such employees, and shall certify the result thereof to such labor organization and to the employer.]*

(e)(1) Upon the filing with the Board, by 30 per centum or more of the employees in a bargaining unit covered by an agreement between their employer and a labor organization made pursuant to section 8(a)(3), of a petition alleging they desire that such authority be rescinded, the Board shall take a secret ballot of the employees in such unit and certify the results thereof to such labor organization and to the employer.

(2) No election shall be conducted pursuant to this subsection in any bargaining unit or any subdivision within which, in the preceding twelve-month period, a valid election shall have been held....

---

* Repealed by Pub. Law 189, 82d Cong., 1st Sess., approved October 22, 1951, which also renumbered the next two subsections and made minor changes in the present subsection (e)(1).—Ed.

PREVENTION OF UNFAIR LABOR PRACTICES

§ **10.** (a) The Board is empowered, as hereinafter provided, to prevent any person from engaging in any unfair labor practice (listed in section 8) affecting commerce. This power shall not be affected by any other means of adjustment or prevention that has been or may be established by agreement, law, or otherwise: ***Provided*, That the Board is empowered by agreement with any agency of any State or Territory to cede to such agency jurisdiction over any cases in any industry (other than mining, manufacturing, communications, and transportation except where predominantly local in character) even though such cases may involve labor disputes affecting commerce, unless the provision of the State or Territorial statute applicable to the determination of such cases by such agency is inconsistent with the corresponding provision of this Act or has received a construction inconsistent therewith.**

(b) Whenever it is charged that any person has engaged in or is engaging in any such unfair labor practice, the Board, or any agent or agency designated by the Board for such purposes, shall have power to issue and cause to be served upon such person a complaint stating the charges in that respect, and containing a notice of hearing before the Board or a member thereof, or before a designated agent or agency, at a place therein fixed, not less than five days after the serving of said complaint: ***Provided*, That no complaint shall issue based upon any unfair labor practice occurring more than six months prior to the filing of the charge with the Board and the service of a copy thereof upon the person against whom such charge is made, unless the person aggrieved thereby was prevented from filing such charge by reason of service in the armed forces, in which event the six-month period shall be computed from the day of his discharge.** Any such complaint may be amended by the member, agent, or agency conducting the hearing or the Board in its discretion at any time prior to the issuance of an order based thereon. The person so complained of shall have the right to file an answer to the original or amended complaint and to appear in person or otherwise and give testimony at the place and time fixed in the complaint. In the discretion of the member, agent, or agency conducting the hearing or the Board, any other person may be allowed to intervene in the said proceeding and to present testimony. [In any such proceeding the rules of evidence prevailing in courts of law or equity shall not be controlling.] **Any such proceeding shall, so far as practicable, be conducted in accordance with the rules of evidence applicable in the district courts of the United States under the rules of civil procedure for the district courts of the United States, adopted by the Supreme Court of the United States pursuant to the Act of June 19, 1934 (U.S.C., title 28, secs. 723-B, 723-C).**

(c) The testimony taken by such member, agent, or agency or the Board shall be reduced to writing and filed with the Board. Thereafter, in its discretion, the Board upon notice may take further testimony or hear argument. If upon [all] **the preponderance of** the testimony taken the Board shall be of the opinion that any person named in the complaint has engaged in or is engaging in any such unfair labor practice, then the Board shall state its findings of fact and shall issue and cause to be served on such person an order requiring such person to cease and desist from such unfair labor practice, and to take such affirmative action including reinstatement of employees with or without back pay, as will effectuate the policies of this Act: *Provided,* **That where an order directs reinstatement of an employee, back pay may be required of the employer or labor organization, as the case may be, responsible for the discrimination suffered by him:** *And provided further,* **That in determining whether a complaint shall issue alleging a violation of section 8(a)(1) or section 8(a)(2), and in deciding such cases, the same regulations and rules of decision shall apply irrespective of whether or not the labor organization affected is affiliated with a labor organization national or international in scope. Such order may further require such person to make reports from time to time showing the extent to which it has complied with the order.** If upon [all] **the preponderance of** the testimony taken the Board shall not be of the opinion that the person named in the complaint has engaged in or is engaging in any such unfair labor practice, then the Board shall state its findings of fact and shall issue an order dismissing the said complaint. **No order of the Board shall require the reinstatement of any individual as an employee who has been suspended or discharged, or the payment to him of any back pay, if such individual was suspended or discharged for cause. In case the evidence is presented before a member of the Board, or before an examiner or examiners thereof, such member, or such examiner or examiners, as the case may be, shall issue and cause to be served on the parties to the proceeding a proposed report, together with a recommended order, which shall be filed with the Board, and if no exceptions are filed within twenty days after service thereof upon such parties, or within such further period as the Board may authorize, such recommended order shall become the order of the Board and become effective as therein prescribed**....

(e) The Board shall have power to petition any court of appeals of the United States, or if all the courts of appeals to which application may be made are in vacation, any district court of the United States, within any circuit or district, respectively, wherein the unfair labor practice in question occurred or wherein such person resides or transacts business, for the enforcement of such order and for appropriate temporary relief or restraining order, and shall file in the court the record in the proceedings, as provided in section 2112 of title 28, United States Code. Upon the filing of such petition, the court shall cause notice thereof to be served upon such person, and thereupon shall have jurisdiction of the proceeding and of the question determined therein, and shall have power to grant such temporary relief or restraining order as it deems just and proper, and to make and enter a decree enforcing, modifying, and enforcing as so modified, or setting aside in whole or in part the order of the Board. No objection that has not been urged before the Board, its member, agent, or agency, shall be considered by the court, unless the failure or neglect to urge such objection shall be excused because of extraordinary circumstances. The findings of the Board with respect to questions of fact if supported by **substantial** evidence **on the record considered as a whole** shall be conclusive. If either party shall apply to the court for leave to adduce additional evidence and shall show to the satisfaction of the court that such additional evidence is material and that there were reasonable grounds for the failure to adduce such evidence in the hearing before the Board, its member, agent, or agency, the court may order such additional evidence to be taken before the Board, its member, agent, or agency, and to be made a part of the record. The Board may modify its findings as to the facts, or make new findings, by reason of additional evidence so taken and filed, and it shall file such modified or new findings, which findings with respect to questions of fact if supported by **substantial** evidence **on the record considered as a whole** shall be conclusive, and shall file its recommendations, if any, for the modification or setting aside of its original order. Upon the filing of the record with it the jurisdiction of the court shall be exclusive and its judgment and decree shall be final, except that the same shall be subject to review by the appropriate United States court of appeals if application was made to the district court as hereinabove provided, and by the Supreme Court of the United States upon writ of certiorari or certification as provided in section 1254 of title 28.

(f) Any person aggrieved by a final order of the Board granting or denying in whole or in part the relief sought may obtain a review of such order in any circuit court of appeals of the United States in the circuit wherein the unfair labor practice in question was alleged to have been engaged in or wherein such person resides or transacts business, or in the United States Court of Appeals for the District of Columbia, by filing in such court a written petition praying that the order of the Board be modified or set aside. A copy of such petition shall be forthwith transmitted by the clerk of the court to the Board, and thereupon the aggrieved party shall file in the court the record in the proceeding, certified by the Board, as provided in section 2112 of title 28, United States Code. Upon the filing of such petition, the court shall proceed in the same manner as in the case of an application by the Board under subsection (e) of this section, and shall have the same jurisdiction to grant to the Board such temporary relief or restraining order as it deems just and proper, and in like manner to make and enter a decree enforcing, modifying, and enforcing as so modified, or setting aside in whole or in part the order of the Board; the findings of the Board with respect to questions of fact if supported by **substantial** evidence **on the record considered as a whole** shall in like manner be conclusive.

(g) The commencement of proceedings under subsection (e) or (f) of this section shall not, unless specifically ordered by the court, operate as a stay of the Board's order.

(h) When granting appropriate temporary relief or a restraining order, or making and entering a decree enforcing, modifying, and enforcing as so modified, or setting aside in whole or in part an order of the Board, as provided in this section, the jurisdiction of courts sitting in equity shall not be limited by the Act entitled "An Act to amend the Judicial Code and to define and limit the jurisdiction of courts sitting in equity, and for other purposes," approved March 23, 1932 (U.S.C., Supp. VII, title 29, secs. 101–115)....

(j) The Board shall have power, upon issuance of a complaint as provided in subsection (b) charging that any person has engaged in or is engaging in an unfair labor practice, to petition any district court of the United States (including the District Court of the United States for the District of Columbia), within any district wherein the unfair labor practice in question is alleged to have occurred or wherein such person resides or transacts business, for appropriate temporary relief or restraining order. Upon the filing of any such petition the court shall cause notice thereof to be served upon such person, and thereupon shall have jurisdiction to grant to the Board such temporary relief or restraining order as it deems just and proper.

(k) Whenever it is charged that any person has engaged in an unfair labor practice within the meaning of paragraph (4)(D) of section 8(b), the Board is empowered and directed to hear and determine the dispute out of which such unfair labor practice shall have arisen, unless, within ten days after notice that such charge has been filed, the parties to such dispute submit to the Board satisfactory evidence that they have adjusted, or agreed upon methods for the voluntary adjustment of, the dispute. Upon compliance by the parties to the dispute with the decision of the Board or upon such voluntary adjustment of the dispute, such charge shall be dismissed.

(*l*) Whenever it is charged that any person has engaged in an unfair labor practice within the meaning of paragraph (4)(A), (B), or (C) of section 8(b), *or section 8(e) or section (b)(7),* **the preliminary investigation of such charge shall be made forthwith and given priority over all other cases except cases of like character in the office where it is filed or to which it is referred. If, after such investigation, the officer or regional attorney to whom the matter may be referred has reasonable cause to believe such charge is**

true and that a complaint should issue, he shall, on behalf of the Board, petition any district court of the United States (including the District Court of the United States for the District of Columbia) within any district where the unfair labor practice in question has occurred, is alleged to have occurred, or wherein such person resides or transacts business, for appropriate injunctive relief pending the final adjudication of the Board with respect to such matter. Upon the filing of any such petition the district court shall have jurisdiction to grant such injunctive relief or temporary restraining order as it deems just and proper, notwithstanding any other provision of law: *Provided further*, That no temporary restraining order shall be issued without notice unless a petition alleges that substantial and irreparable injury to the charging party will be unavoidable and such temporary restraining order shall be effective for no longer than five days and will become void at the expiration of such period [-]: *Provided further, That such officer or regional attorney shall not apply for any restraining order under section 8(b)(7) if a charge against the employer under section 8(a)(2) has been filed and after the preliminary investigation, he has reasonable cause to believe that such charge is true and that a complaint should issue.* Upon filing of any such petition the courts shall cause notice thereof to be served upon any person involved in the charge and such person, including the charging party, shall be given an opportunity to appear by counsel and present any relevant testimony: *Provided further*, That for the purposes of this subsection district courts shall be deemed to have jurisdiction of a labor organization (1) in the district in which such organization maintains its principal office, or (2) in any district in which its duly authorized officers or agents are engaged in promoting or protecting the interests of employee members. The service of legal process upon such officer or agent shall constitute service upon the labor organization and make such organization a party to the suit. In situations where such relief is appropriate the procedure specified herein shall apply to charges with respect to section 8(b)(4)(D).

(m) Whenever it is charged that any person has engaged in an unfair labor practice within the meaning of subsection (a)(3) or (b)(2) of section 8, such charge shall be given priority over all other cases except cases of like character in the office where it is filed or to which it is referred and cases given priority under subsection (l).

INVESTIGATORY POWERS

§ 11.   For the purpose of all hearings and investigations, which, in the opinion of the Board, are necessary and proper for the exercise of the powers vested in it by section 9 and section 10—

(1) The Board, or its duly authorized agents or agencies, shall at all reasonable times have access to, for the purpose of examination, and the

right to copy any evidence of any person being investigated or proceeded against that relates to any matter under investigation or in question. The Board, or any member thereof, shall upon application of any party to such proceedings, forthwith issue to such party subpenas requiring the attendance and testimony of witnesses or the production of any evidence in such proceeding or investigation requested in such application. Within five days after the service of a subpena on any person requiring the production of any evidence in his possession or under his control, such person may petition the Board to revoke, and the Board shall revoke, such subpena if in its opinion the evidence whose production is required does not relate to any matter under investigation, or any matter in question in such proceedings, or if in its opinion such subpena does not describe with sufficient particularity the evidence whose production is required. Any member of the Board, or any agent or agency designated by the Board for such purposes, may administer oaths and affirmations, examine witnesses, and receive evidence. Such attendance of witnesses and the production of such evidence may be required from any place in the United States or any Territory or possession thereof, at any designated place of hearing.

(2) In case of contumacy or refusal to obey a subpena issued to any person, any district court of the United States or the United States courts of any Territory or possession, or the District Court of the United States for the District of Columbia, within the jurisdiction of which the inquiry is carried on or within the jurisdiction of which said person guilty of contumacy or refusal to obey is found or resides or transacts business, upon application by the Board shall have jurisdiction to issue to such person an order requiring such person to appear before the Board, its member, agent, or agency, there to produce evidence if so ordered, or there to give testimony touching the matter under investigation or in question; and any failure to obey such order of the court may be punished by said court as a contempt thereof. . . .

§ 12. Any person who shall willfully resist, prevent, impede, or interfere with any member of the Board or any of its agents or agencies in the performance of duties pursuant to this Act shall be punished by a fine of not more than $5,000 or by imprisonment for not more than one year, or both.

LIMITATIONS

§ 13. Nothing in this Act, **except as specifically provided for herein,** shall be construed so as either to interfere with or impede or diminish in any way the right to strike, **or to affect the limitations or qualifications on that right.**

§ 14. (a) **Nothing herein shall prohibit any individual employed as a supervisor from becoming or remaining a member of a labor organization, but no employer subject to this Act shall be compelled to deem individuals defined herein as supervisors as** employees for the purpose of any law, either national or local, relating to collective bargaining.

(b) Nothing in this Act shall be construed as authorizing the execution or application of agreements requiring membership in a labor organization as a condition of employment in any State or Territory in which such execution or application is prohibited by State or Territorial law.

(c)(1) The Board, in its discretion, may, by rule of decision or by published rules adopted pursuant to the Administrative Procedure Act, decline to assert jurisdiction over any labor dispute involving any class or category of employers, where, in the opinion of the Board, the effect of such labor dispute on commerce is not sufficiently substantial to warrant the exercise of its jurisdiction: Provided, *That the Board shall not decline to assert jurisdiction over any labor dispute over which it would assert jurisdiction under the standards prevailing upon August 1, 1959.*

(2) Nothing in this Act shall be deemed to prevent or bar any agency or the courts of any State or Territory (including the Commonwealth of Puerto Rico, Guam, and the Virgin Islands), from assuming and asserting jurisdiction over labor disputes over which the Board declines, pursuant to paragraph (1) of this subsection, to assert jurisdiction . . . .

INDIVIDUALS WITH RELIGIOUS CONVICTIONS

§ 19. ANY EMPLOYEE [OF A HEALTH CARE INSTITUTION]* WHO IS A MEMBER OF AND ADHERES TO ESTABLISHED AND TRADITIONAL TENETS OR TEACHINGS OF A BONA FIDE RELIGION, BODY, OR SECT WHICH HAS HISTORICALLY HELD CONSCIENTIOUS OBJECTIONS TO JOINING OR FINANCIALLY SUPPORTING LABOR ORGANIZATIONS SHALL NOT BE REQUIRED TO JOIN OR FINANCIALLY SUPPORT ANY LABOR ORGANIZATION AS A CONDITION OF EMPLOYMENT; EXCEPT THAT SUCH EMPLOYEE MAY BE REQUIRED IN A CONTRACT BETWEEN SUCH EMPLOYEES' EMPLOYER AND A LABOR ORGANIZATION IN LIEU OF PERIODIC DUES AND INITIATION FEES, TO PAY SUMS EQUAL TO SUCH DUES AND INITIATION FEES TO A NONRELIGIOUS, NONLABOR ORGANIZATION CHARITABLE FUND EXEMPT FROM TAXATION UNDER SECTION 501(c)(3) OF TITLE 26 OF THE INTERNAL REVENUE CODE, CHOSEN BY SUCH EMPLOYEE FROM A LIST OF AT LEAST THREE SUCH FUNDS, DESIGNATED IN [A] SUCH CONTRACT [BETWEEN SUCH INSTITUTION AND A LABOR ORGANIZATION] OR IF THE CONTRACT FAILS TO DESIGNATE SUCH FUNDS, THEN TO ANY SUCH FUNDS CHOSEN BY THE EMPLOYEE. IF SUCH EMPLOYEE WHO HOLDS CONSCIENTIOUS OBJECTIONS PURSUANT TO THIS

---

* Public Law 96-563 (H.R.4774), 94 Stat. 3452, approved December 24, 1980, amended this section. Deleted language is in brackets; new language added by the amendment is underscored.—ED.

SECTION REQUESTS THE LABOR ORGANIZATION TO USE THE GRIEVANCE–ARBITRATION PROCEDURE ON THE EMPLOYEE'S BE-HALF, THE LABOR ORGANIZATION IS AUTHORIZED TO CHARGE THE EMPLOYEE FOR THE REASONABLE COST OF USING SUCH PROCEDURE.

TITLE II. CONCILIATION OF LABOR DISPUTES; NATIONAL EMERGENCIES

§ 201.   That it is the policy of the United States that—

(a) sound and stable industrial peace and the advancement of the general welfare, health, and safety of the Nation and of the best interests of employers and employees can most satisfactorily be secured by the settlement of issues between employers and employees through the processes of conference and collective bargaining between employers and the representatives of their employees;

(b) the settlement of issues between employers and employees through collective bargaining may be advanced by making available full and adequate governmental facilities for conciliation, mediation, and voluntary arbitration to aid and encourage employers and the representatives of their employees to reach and maintain agreements concerning rates of pay, hours, and working conditions, and to make all reasonable efforts to settle their differences by mutual agreement reached through conferences and collective bargaining or by such methods as may be provided for in any applicable agreement for the settlement of disputes; and

(c) certain controversies which arise between parties to collective-bargaining agreements may be avoided or minimized by making available full and adequate governmental facilities for furnishing assistance to employers and the representatives of their employees in formulating for inclusion within such agreements provision for adequate notice of any proposed changes in the terms of such agreements, for the final adjustment of grievances or questions regarding the application or interpretation of such agreements, and other provisions designed to prevent the subsequent arising of such controversies.

§ 202.   (a) There is created an independent agency to be known as the Federal Mediation and Conciliation Service (herein referred to as the "Service," except that for sixty days after June 23, 1947, such term shall refer to the Conciliation Service of the Department of Labor). The Service shall be under the direction of a Federal Mediation and Conciliation Director (hereinafter referred to as the "Director"), who shall be appointed by the President by and with the advice and consent of the Senate. The Director shall not engage in any other business, vocation, or employment.

(b) The Director is authorized, subject to the civil service laws, to appoint such clerical and other personnel as may be necessary for the execution of the functions of the Service, and shall fix their compensation in accordance with the Classification Act of 1949, and may, without regard to the provisions of the civil service laws, appoint such conciliators and mediators as may be necessary to carry out the functions of the Service. The Director is authorized to make such expenditures for supplies, facilities, and services as he deems necessary. Such expenditures shall be allowed and paid upon presentation of itemized vouchers therefor approved by the Director or by any employee designated by him for that purpose.

(c) The principal office of the Service shall be in the District of Columbia, but the Director may establish regional offices convenient to localities in which labor controversies are likely to arise. The Director may by order, subject to revocation at any time, delegate any authority and discretion conferred upon him by this chapter to any regional director, or other officer or employee of the Service. The Director may establish suitable procedures for cooperation with State and local mediation agencies. The Director shall make an annual report in writing to Congress at the end of the fiscal year....

FUNCTIONS OF THE SERVICE

§ 203. (a) It shall be the duty of the Service, in order to prevent or minimize interruptions of the free flow of commerce growing out of labor disputes, to assist parties to labor disputes in industries affecting commerce to settle such disputes through conciliation and mediation.

(b) The Service may proffer its services in any labor dispute in any industry affecting commerce, either upon its own motion or upon the request of one or more of the parties to the dispute, whenever in its judgment such dispute threatens to cause a substantial interruption of commerce. The Director and the Service are directed to avoid attempting to mediate disputes which would have only a minor effect on interstate commerce if State or other conciliation services are available to the parties. Whenever the Service does proffer its services in any dispute, it shall be the duty of the Service promptly to put itself in communication with the parties and to use its best efforts, by mediation and conciliation, to bring them to agreement.

(c) If the Director is not able to bring the parties to agreement by conciliation within a reasonable time, he shall seek to induce the parties voluntarily to seek other means of settling the dispute without resort to strike, lock-out, or other coercion, including submission to the employees in the bargaining unit of the employer's last offer of settlement for approval or rejection in a secret ballot. The failure or refusal of either party to agree to any procedure suggested by the Director shall not be deemed a violation of any duty or obligation imposed by this Act.

(d) Final adjustment by a method agreed upon by the parties is hereby declared to be the desirable method for settlement of grievance disputes arising over the application or interpretation of an existing collective-bargaining agreement. The Service is directed to make its conciliation and mediation services available in the settlement of such grievance disputes only as a last resort and in exceptional cases.

(e) The Service is authorized and directed to encourage and support the establishment and operation of joint labor management activities conducted by plant, area, and industrywide committees designed to improve labor management relationships, job security and organizational effectiveness, in accordance with the provisions of section 205A. . . . *

§ 204. (a) In order to prevent or minimize interruptions of the free flow of commerce growing out of labor disputes, employers and employees and their representatives, in any industry affecting commerce, shall—

(1) exert every reasonable effort to make and maintain agreements concerning rates of pay, hours, and working conditions, including provision for adequate notice of any proposed change in the terms of such agreements;

(2) whenever a dispute arises over the terms or application of a collective-bargaining agreement and a conference is requested by a party or prospective party thereto, arrange promptly for such a conference to be held and endeavor in such conference to settle such dispute expeditiously; and

(3) in case such dispute is not settled by conference, participate fully and promptly in such meetings as may be undertaken by the Service under this Act for the purpose of aiding in a settlement of the dispute.

§ 205. (a) There is created a National Labor–Management Panel which shall be composed of twelve members appointed by the President, six of whom shall be selected from among persons outstanding in the field of management and six of whom shall be selected from among persons outstanding in the field of labor. Each member shall hold office for a term of three years, except that any member appointed to fill a vacancy occurring prior to the expiration of the term for which his predecessor was appointed shall be appointed for the remainder of such term, and the terms of office of the members first taking office shall expire, as designated by the President at the time of appointment, four at the end of the first year, four at the end of the second year, and four at the end of the third year after the date of appointment. Members of the panel, when serving on business of the panel, shall be paid compensation at the rate of $25 per day, and shall also be entitled to receive an allowance for actual and necessary travel and subsistence expenses while so serving away from their places of residence.

(b) It shall be the duty of the panel, at the request of the Director, to advise in the avoidance of industrial controversies and the manner in which mediation and voluntary adjustment shall be administered, particularly with reference to controversies affecting the general welfare of the country.

---

* Added by Congress in 1978, by Pub.L. 95–524, § 6(c)(1), 92 Stat. 2020.—Ed.

§ 205A. (a)(1) The Service is authorized and directed to provide assistance in the establishment and operation of plant, area and industry-wide labor management committees which—

(A) have been organized jointly by employers and labor organizations representing employees in that plant, area, or industry; and

(B) are established for the purpose of improving labor management relationships, job security, organizational effectiveness, enhancing economic development or involving workers in decisions affecting their jobs including improving communication with respect to subjects of mutual interest and concern.

(2) The Service is authorized and directed to enter into contracts and to make grants, where necessary or appropriate, to fulfill its responsibilities under this section.

(b)(1) No grant may be made, no contract may be entered into and no other assistance may be provided under the provisions of this section to a plant labor management committee unless the employees in that plant are represented by a labor organization and there is in effect at that plant a collective bargaining agreement.

(2) No grant may be made, no contract may be entered into and no other assistance may be provided under the provisions of this section to an area or industrywide labor management committee unless its participants include any labor organizations certified or recognized as the representative of the employees of an employer participating in such committee. Nothing in this clause shall prohibit participation in an area or industrywide committee by an employer whose employees are not represented by a labor organization.

(3) No grant may be made under the provisions of this section to any labor management committee which the Service finds to have as one of its purposes the discouragement of the exercise of rights contained in section 7 of the National Labor Relations Act, or the interference with collective bargaining in any plant, or industry . . . . *

NATIONAL EMERGENCIES

§ 206. Whenever in the opinion of the President of the United States, a threatened or actual strike or lock-out affecting an entire industry or a substantial part thereof engaged in trade, commerce, transportation, transmission, or communication among the several States or with foreign nations, or engaged in the production of goods for commerce, will, if permitted to occur or to continue, imperil the national health or safety, he may appoint a board of inquiry to inquire into the issues involved in the dispute and to make a written report to him within such time as he shall prescribe. Such report shall include a statement of the facts with respect to the dispute, including each party's statement of its position but shall not

* Added by Congress in 1978, by Pub.L. 95–524, § 6(2)(c), 92 Stat. 2020.—Ed.

contain any recommendations. The President shall file a copy of such report with the Service and shall make its contents available to the public.

§ **207.** (a) A board of inquiry shall be composed of a chairman and such other members as the President shall determine, and shall have power to sit and act in any place within the United States and to conduct such hearings either in public or in private, as it may deem necessary or proper, to ascertain the facts with respect to the causes and circumstances of the dispute. . . .

§ **208.** (a) Upon receiving a report from a board of inquiry the President may direct the Attorney General to petition any district court of the United States having jurisdiction of the parties to enjoin such strike or lock-out or the continuing thereof, and if the court finds that such threatened or actual strike or lock-out—

> (i) affects an entire industry or a substantial part thereof engaged in trade, commerce, transportation, transmission, or communication among the several States or with foreign nations, or engaged in the production of goods for commerce; and

> (ii) if permitted to occur or to continue, will imperil the national health or safety, it shall have jurisdiction to enjoin any such strike or lock-out, or the continuing thereof, and to make such other orders as may be appropriate.

(b) In any case, the provisions of the Act of March 23, 1932, entitled "An Act to amend the Judicial Code and to define and limit the jurisdiction of courts sitting in equity, and for other purposes," shall not be applicable.

(c) The order or orders of the court shall be subject to review by the appropriate United States court of appeals and by the Supreme Court upon writ of certiorari or certification as provided in sections 239 and 240 of the Judicial Code, as amended (U.S.C., title 29, secs. 346 and 347).

§ **209.** (a) Whenever a district court has issued an order under section 208 enjoining acts or practices which imperil or threaten to imperil the national health or safety, it shall be the duty of the parties to the labor dispute giving rise to such order to make every effort to adjust and settle their differences, with the assistance of the Service created by this Act. Neither party shall be under any duty to accept, in whole or in part, any proposal of settlement made by the Service.

(b) Upon the issuance of such order, the President shall reconvene the board of inquiry which has previously reported with respect to the dispute. At the end of a sixty-day period (unless the dispute has been settled by that time), the board of inquiry shall report to the President the current position of the parties and the efforts which have been made for settlement, and shall include a statement by each party of its position and a statement of the employer's last offer of settlement. The President shall make such report available to the public. The National Labor Relations Board, within the succeeding fifteen days, shall take a secret ballot of the employees of each employer involved in the dispute on the question of whether they wish to accept the final offer of settlement made by their employer as stated by him and shall certify the results thereof to the Attorney General within five days thereafter.

§ 210.　Upon the certification of the results of such ballot or upon a settlement being reached, whichever happens sooner, the Attorney General shall move the court to discharge the injunction, which motion shall then be granted and the injunction discharged.　When such motion is granted, the President shall submit to the Congress a full and comprehensive report of the proceedings, including the findings of the board of inquiry and the ballot taken by the National Labor Relations Board, together with such recommendations as he may see fit to make for consideration and appropriate action.

COMPILATION OF COLLECTIVE BARGAINING AGREEMENTS, ETC.

§ 211.　(a) For the guidance and information of interested representatives of employers, employees, and the general public, the Bureau of Labor Statistics of the Department of Labor shall maintain a file of copies of all available collective bargaining agreements and other available agreements and actions thereunder settling or adjusting labor disputes.　Such file shall be open to inspection under appropriate conditions prescribed by the Secretary of Labor, except that no specific information submitted in confidence shall be disclosed.

(b) The Bureau of Labor Statistics in the Department of Labor is authorized to furnish upon request of the Service, or employers, employees, or their representatives, all available data and factual information which may aid in the settlement of any labor dispute, except that no specific information submitted in confidence shall be disclosed.

EXEMPTION OF RAILWAY LABOR ACT

§ 212.　The provisions of this title shall not be applicable with respect to any matter which is subject to the provisions of the Railway Labor Act, as amended from time to time.

CONCILIATION OF LABOR DISPUTES IN THE HEALTH CARE INDUSTRY

§ 213.　(a) IF, IN THE OPINION OF THE DIRECTOR OF THE FEDERAL MEDIATION AND CONCILIATION SERVICE A THREATENED OR ACTUAL STRIKE OR LOCKOUT AFFECTING A HEALTH CARE INSTITUTION WILL, IF PERMITTED TO OCCUR OR TO CONTINUE, SUBSTANTIALLY INTERRUPT THE DELIVERY OF HEALTH CARE IN THE LOCALITY CONCERNED, THE DIRECTOR MAY FURTHER ASSIST IN THE RESOLUTION OF THE IMPASSE BY ESTABLISHING WITHIN 30 DAYS AFTER THE NOTICE TO THE FEDERAL MEDIATION AND CONCILIATION SERVICE UNDER CLAUSE (A) OF

THE LAST SENTENCE OF SECTION 8(d) (WHICH IS REQUIRED BY CLAUSE (3) OF SUCH SECTION 8(d)), OR WITHIN 10 DAYS AFTER THE NOTICE UNDER CLAUSE (B), AN IMPARTIAL BOARD OF INQUIRY TO INVESTIGATE THE ISSUES INVOLVED IN THE DISPUTE AND TO MAKE A WRITTEN REPORT THEREON TO THE PARTIES WITHIN FIFTEEN (15) DAYS AFTER THE ESTABLISHMENT OF SUCH A BOARD. THE WRITTEN REPORT SHALL CONTAIN THE FINDINGS OF FACT TOGETHER WITH THE BOARD'S RECOMMENDATIONS FOR SETTLING THE DISPUTE, WITH THE OBJECTIVE OF ACHIEVING A PROMPT, PEACEFUL AND JUST SETTLEMENT OF THE DISPUTE. EACH SUCH BOARD SHALL BE COMPOSED OF SUCH NUMBER OF INDIVIDUALS AS THE DIRECTOR MAY DEEM DESIRABLE. NO MEMBER APPOINTED UNDER THIS SECTION SHALL HAVE ANY INTEREST OR INVOLVEMENT IN THE HEALTH CARE INSTITUTIONS OR THE EMPLOYEE ORGANIZATIONS INVOLVED IN THE DISPUTE. . . .

TITLE III. SUITS BY AND AGAINST LABOR ORGANIZATIONS

§ 301. (a) Suits for violation of contracts between an employer and a labor organization representing employees in an industry affecting commerce as defined in this Act, or between any such labor organizations, may be brought in any district court of the United States having jurisdiction of the parties, without respect to the amount in controversy or without regard to the citizenship of the parties.

(b) Any labor organization which represents employees in an industry affecting commerce as defined in this Act and any employer whose activities affect commerce as defined in this Act shall be bound by the acts of its agents. Any such labor organization may sue or be sued as an entity and in behalf of the employees whom it represents in the courts of the United States. Any money judgment against a labor organization in a district court of the United States shall be enforceable only against the organization as an entity and against its assets, and shall not be enforceable against any individual member or his assets.

(c) For the purposes of actions and proceedings by or against labor organizations in the district courts of the United States, district courts shall be deemed to have jurisdiction of a labor organization (1) in the district in which such organization maintains its principal office, or (2) in any district in which its duly authorized officers or agents are engaged in representing or acting for employee members.

(d) The service of summons, subpena, or other legal process of any court of the United States upon an officer or agent of a labor organization, in his capacity as such, shall constitute service upon the labor organization.

(e) For the purposes of this section, in determining whether any person is acting as an "agent" of another person so as to make such other person responsible for his acts, the question of whether the specific acts performed were actually authorized or subsequently ratified shall not be controlling.

RESTRICTIONS ON PAYMENTS TO EMPLOYEE REPRESENTA-TIVES*

§ 302. (a) It shall be unlawful for any employer or *association of employers or any person who acts as a labor relations expert, adviser, or consultant to an employer or who acts in the interest of an employer to pay, lend,* or deliver, or [to] agree to pay, *lend, or deliver, any money or other thing of value—*

(1) to any representative of any of his employees who are employed in an industry affecting commerce[.]; *or*

(2) *to any labor organization, or any officer or employee thereof, which represents, seeks to represent, or would admit to membership, any of the employees of such employer who are employed in an industry affecting commerce; or*

(3) *to any employee or group or committee of employees of such employer employed in an industry affecting commerce in excess of their normal compensation for the purpose of causing such employee or group or committee directly or indirectly to influence any other employees in the exercise of the right to organize and bargain collectively through representatives of their own choosing; or*

(4) *to any officer or employee of a labor organization engaged in an industry affecting commerce with intent to influence him in respect to any of his actions, decisions, or duties as a representative of employees or as such officer or employee of such labor organization,*

(b)(1) It shall be unlawful for any [representative of any employees who are employed in an industry affecting commerce] *person to request, demand,* [to] *receive, or accept, or [to] agree to* receive or accept *[from the employer of such employees]* any payment, loan, or delivery of any money or other thing of value[.] prohibited by subsection (a) of this section.

(2) *It shall be unlawful for any labor organization, or for any person acting as an officer, agent, representative, or employee of such labor organization, to demand or accept from the operator of any motor vehicle (as defined in part II of the Interstate Commerce Act) employed in the transportation of property in commerce, or the employer of any such operator, any money or other thing of value payable to such organization or to an officer, agent, representative or employee thereof as a fee or charge for the unloading, or in connection with the unloading, of the cargo of such vehicle: **Provided**, That nothing in this paragraph shall be construed to make*

* Unless otherwise indicated, the provisions of §§ 302 and 303 contained in the LMRA are in roman type below; additions to those sections made by the LMRDA appear in italics; and deletions, in brackets.—ED.

unlawful any payment by an employer to any of his employees as compensation for their services as employees.

(c) The provisions of this section shall not be applicable (1) [with] *in* respect to any money or other thing of value payable by an employer *to any of his employees whose established duties include acting openly for such employer in matters of labor relations or personnel administration or to any representative of his employees, or to any officer or employee of a labor organization,* who is also an employee or former employee of such employer, as compensation for, or by reason of, his service[s] as an employee of such employer; (2) with respect to the payment or delivery of any money or other thing of value in satisfaction of a judgment of any court or a decision or award of an arbitrator or impartial chairman or in compromise, adjustment, settlement, or release of any claim, complaint, grievance, or dispute in the absence of fraud or duress; (3) with respect to the sale or purchase of an article or commodity at the prevailing market price in the regular course of business; (4) with respect to money deducted from the wages of employees in payment of membership dues in a labor organization: Provided, That the employer has received from each employee, on whose account such deductions are made, a written assignment which shall not be irrevocable for a period of more than one year, or beyond the termination date of the applicable collective agreement, whichever occurs sooner; [or] (5) with respect to money or other thing of value paid to a trust fund established by such representative, for the sole and exclusive benefit of the employees of such employer, and their families and dependents (or of such employees, families, and dependents jointly with the employees of other employers making similar payments, and their families and dependents): Provided, That (A) such payments are held in trust for the purpose of paying, either from principal or income or both, for the benefit of employees, their families and dependents, for medical or hospital care, pensions on retirement or death of employees, compensation for injuries or illness resulting from occupational activity or insurance to provide any of the foregoing, or unemployment benefits or life insurance, disability and sickness insurance, or accident insurance; (B) the detailed basis on which such payments are to be made is specified in a written agreement with the employer, and employees and employers are equally represented in the administration of such fund, together with such neutral persons as the representatives of [the] employers and the representatives of employees may agree upon and in the event the employer and employee groups deadlock on the administration of such fund and there are no neutral persons empowered to break such deadlock, such agreement provides that the two groups shall agree on an impartial umpire to decide such dispute, or in event of their failure to agree within a reasonable length of time, an impartial umpire to decide such dispute shall, on petition of either group, be appointed by the district court of the United States for the district where the trust fund has its principal office, and shall also contain provisions for an annual audit of the trust fund, a statement of the results of which shall be available for inspection by interested persons at the principal office of the trust fund and at such other places as may be designated in such written agreement; and (C) such payments as are intended to be used for the purpose of providing pensions or annuities for employees are made to a separate trust which provides that the funds held therein cannot be used for any purpose other than paying such pensions or annuities[.]; *or (6) with respect to money or other thing of value paid by any employer to a trust fund established by such representative for the purpose of pooled vacation, holiday, severance or similar benefits, or defraying costs of apprenticeship or other training programs:* **Provided***, That the requirements of clause (B) of the proviso to clause (5) of this subsection shall apply to such trust funds;*

or (7) with respect to money or other thing of value paid by any employer to a pooled or individual trust fund established by such representative for the purpose of (A) scholarships for the benefit of employees, their families, and dependents for study at educational institutions, (B) child care centers for pre-school and school age dependents: *Provided,* That no labor organization or employer shall be required to bargain on the establishment of any such trust fund, and refusal to do so shall not constitute an unfair labor practice: *Provided further,* That the requirements of clause (B) of the proviso to clause (5) of this subsection shall apply to such trust funds;*

or (8) with respect to money or any other thing of value paid by any employer to a trust fund established by such representative for the purpose of defraying the costs of legal services for employees, their families, and dependents for counsel or plan of their choice: *Provided further,* That the requirements of clause (B) of the proviso to clause (5) of this subsection shall apply to such trust funds: *Provided further,* That no such legal services shall be furnished: (A) to initiate any proceeding directed (i) against any such employer or its officers or agents except in workman's compensation cases, or (ii) against such labor organization, or its parent or subordinate bodies, or their officers or agents, or (iii) against any other employer or labor organization, or their officers or agents, in any matter arising under the National Labor Relations Act, as amended, or this Act; and (B) in any proceeding where a labor organization would be prohibited from defraying the costs of legal services by the provisions of the Labor–Management Reporting and Disclosure Act of 1959;** or

(9) with respect to money or other things of value paid by an employer to a plant, area or industry-wide labor management committee established for one or more of the purposes set forth in section 5(b) of the Labor–Management Cooperation Act of 1978.***

---

* Clause (7) of § 302(c) was added by Pub.L. 91–86, 83 Stat. 133 (1969).—Ed.

** Clause (8) of § 302 was added by Pub.L. 93–95, 87 Stat. 314 (1973).—Ed.

*** Clause (9) of § 302 was added by Pub.L. 95–524, 92 Stat. 2021 (1978).—Ed.

(d)(1) Any person who participates in a transaction involving a payment, loan, or delivery of money or other thing of value to a labor organization in payment of membership dues or to a joint labor-management trust fund as defined by clause (B) of the proviso to clause (5) of subsection (c) of this section or to a plant, area, or industry-wide labor-management committee that is received and used by such labor organization, trust fund, or committee, which transaction does not satisfy all the applicable requirements of subsections (c)(4) through (c)(9) of this section, and willfully and with intent to benefit himself or to benefit other persons he knows are not permitted to receive a payment, loan, money, or other thing of value under subsections (c)(4) through (c)(9) violates this subsection, shall, upon conviction thereof, be guilty of a felony and be subject to a fine of not more than $15,000, or imprisoned for not more than five years, or both; but if the value of the amount of money or thing of value involved in any violation of the provisions of this section does not exceed $1,000, such person shall be guilty of a misdemeanor and be subject to a fine of not more than $10,000, or imprisoned for not more than one year, or both.

(2) Except for violations involving transactions covered by subsection (d)(1) of this section, any person who willfully violates this section shall, upon conviction thereof, be guilty of a felony and be subject to a fine of not more than $15,000, or imprisoned for not more than five years, or both; but if the value of the amount of money or thing of value involved in any violation of the provisions of this section does not exceed $1,000, such person shall be guilty of a misdemeanor and be subject to a fine of not more than $10,000, or imprisoned for not more than one year, or both.*

(e) The district courts of the United States and the United States courts of the Territories and possessions shall have jurisdiction, for cause shown, and subject to the provisions of section 17 (relating to notice to opposite party) of the Act entitled "An Act to supplement existing laws against unlawful restraints and monopolies, and for other purposes," approved October 15, 1914, as amended (U.S.C., title 28, sec. 381), to restrain violations of this section, without regard to the provisions of sections 6 and 20 of such Act of October 15, 1914, as amended (U.S.C., title 15, sec. 17, and title 29, sec. 52), and the provisions of the Act entitled "An Act to amend the Judicial Code and to define and limit the jurisdiction of courts sitting in equity, and for other purposes," approved March 23, 1932 (U.S.C., title 29, secs. 101–115). . . .

BOYCOTTS AND OTHER UNLAWFUL COMBINATIONS

§ 303. (a) It shall be unlawful, for the purpose[s] of this section only, in an industry or activity affecting commerce, for any labor organization to

---

* Section 302(d) was amended by Pub.L. 98–473, 98 Stat. 2131 (1984), resulting in subsections d(1) and (2).—ED.

engage in *any activity or conduct defined as an unfair labor practice in section 8(b)(4) of the National Labor Relations Act, as amended.*

(b) Whoever shall be injured in his business or property by reason of any violation of subsection (a) may sue therefor in any district court of the United States subject to the limitations and provisions of section 301 hereof without respect to the amount in controversy, or in any other court having jurisdiction of the parties, and shall recover the damages by him sustained and the cost of the suit.....

TITLE IV. CREATION OF JOINT COMMITTEE TO STUDY AND REPORT ON BASIC PROBLEMS AFFECTING FRIENDLY LABOR RELATIONS AND PRODUCTIVITY

TITLE V. DEFINITIONS

§ **501.** When used in this Act—

(1) The term "industry affecting commerce" means any industry or activity in commerce or in which a labor dispute would burden or obstruct commerce or tend to burden or obstruct commerce or the free flow of commerce.

(2) The term "strike" includes any strike or other concerted stoppage of work by employees (including a stoppage by reason of the expiration of a collective-bargaining agreement) and any concerted slow-down or other concerted interruption of operations by employees.

(3) The terms "commerce," "labor disputes," "employer," "employee," "labor organization," "representative," "person," and "supervisor" shall have the same meaning as when used in the National Labor Relations Act as amended by this Act.

SAVING PROVISION

§ **502.** Nothing in this Act shall be construed to require an individual employee to render labor or service without his consent, nor shall anything in this Act be construed to make the quitting of his labor by an individual employee an illegal act; nor shall any court issue any process to compel the performance by an individual employee of such labor or service, without his consent; nor shall the quitting of labor by an employee or employees in good faith because of abnormally dangerous conditions for work at the place of employment of such employee or employees be deemed a strike under this Act.

SEPARABILITY

§ **503.** If any provision of this Act, or the application of such provision to any person or circumstance, shall be held invalid, the remainder of this Act, or the application of such provision to persons or circumstances other than those as to which it is held invalid, shall not be affected thereby.

*

LABOR–MANAGEMENT REPORTING AND DISCLOSURE ACT*

73 Stat. 519 (1959); as amended by Pub. L. No. 89-216, 89th Cong., 1st Sess., 1965, 79 Stat. 888; 29 U.S.C. §§ 401-531

SHORT TITLE

§ 1. This Act may be cited as the "Labor–Management Reporting and Disclosure Act of 1959."

DECLARATION OF FINDINGS, PURPOSES, AND POLICY

§ 2. (a) The Congress finds that, in the public interest, it continues to be the responsibility of the Federal Government to protect employees' rights to organize, choose their own representatives, bargain collectively, and otherwise engage in concerted activities for their mutual aid or protection; that the relations between employers and labor organizations and the millions of workers they represent have a substantial impact on the commerce of the Nation; and that in order to accomplish the objective of a free flow of commerce it is essential that labor organizations, employers, and their officials adhere to the highest standards of responsibility and ethical conduct in administering the affairs of their organizations, particularly as they affect labor-management relations.

(b) The Congress further finds, from recent investigations in the labor and management fields, that there have been a number of instances of breach of trust, corruption, disregard of the rights of individual employees, and other failures to observe high standards of responsibility and ethical conduct which require further and supplementary legislation that will afford necessary protection of the rights and interests of employees and the public generally as they relate to the activities of labor organizations, employers, labor relations consultants, and their officers and representatives.

(c) The Congress, therefore, further finds and declares that the enactment of this chapter is necessary to eliminate or prevent improper practices on the part of labor organizations, employers, labor relations consultants, and their officers and representatives which distort and defeat the policies of the Labor Management Relations Act, 1947, as amended, and the Railway Labor Act, as amended, and have the tendency or necessary effect of burdening or obstructing commerce by (1) impairing the efficiency, safety, or operation of the instrumentalities of commerce; (2) occurring in the current of commerce; (3) materially affecting, restraining, or controlling the flow of raw materials or manufactured or processed goods into or from the channels of commerce, or the prices of such materials or goods in

---

* The 1959 LMRDA, in Title VII, § 201(d) and (e), and § 505, amends the 1935 NLRA and the 1947 LMRA. Since this Statutory Supplement has incorporated these amendments in the appropriate sections of the earlier legislation, they are omitted here.—ED.

commerce; or (4) causing diminution of employment and wages in such volume as substantially to impair or disrupt the market for goods flowing into or from the channels of commerce.

DEFINITIONS

§ 3. For the purposes of this title I, II, III, IV, V (except section 505j), and VI of this Act—

(a) "Commerce" means trade, traffic, commerce, transportation, transmission, or communication among the several States or between any State and any place outside thereof.

(b) "State" includes any State of the United States, the District of Columbia, Puerto Rico, the Virgin Islands, American Samoa, Guam, Wake Island, the Canal Zone, and Outer Continental Shelf lands defined in the Outer Continental Shelf Lands Act (43 U.S.C.A. § 1331-1343).

(c) "Industry affecting commerce" means any activity, business, or industry in commerce or in which a labor dispute would hinder or obstruct commerce or the free flow of commerce and includes any activity or industry "affecting commerce" within the meaning of the Labor Management Relations Act, 1947, as amended, or the Railway Labor Act, as amended.

(d) "Person" includes one or more individuals, labor organizations, partnerships, associations, corporations, legal representatives, mutual companies, joint-stock companies, trusts, unincorporated organizations, trustees, trustees in bankruptcy, or receivers.

(e) "Employer" means any employer or any group or association of employers engaged in an industry affecting commerce (1) which is, with respect to employees engaged in an industry affecting commerce, an employer within the meaning of any law of the United States relating to the employment of any employees or (2) which may deal with any labor organization concerning grievances, labor disputes, wages, rates of pay, hours of employment, or conditions of work, and includes any person acting directly or indirectly as an employer or as an agent of an employer in relation to an employee but does not include the United States or any corporation wholly owned by the Government of the United States or any State or political subdivision thereof.

(f) "Employee" means any individual employed by an employer, and includes any individual whose work has ceased as a consequence of, or in connection with, any current labor dispute or because of any unfair labor practice or because of exclusion or expulsion from a labor organization in any manner or for any reason inconsistent with the requirements of this Act.

(g) "Labor dispute" includes any controversy concerning terms, tenure, or conditions of employment, or concerning the association or representation of persons in negotiating, fixing, maintaining, changing, or seeking to arrange terms or conditions of employment, regardless of whether the disputants stand in the proximate relation of employer and employee.

(h) "Trusteeship" means any receivership, trusteeship, or other method of supervision or control whereby a labor organization suspends the autonomy otherwise available to a subordinate body under its constitution or bylaws.

(i) "Labor organization" means a labor organization engaged in an industry affecting commerce and includes any organization of any kind, any agency, or employee representation committee, group, association, or plan so engaged in which employees participate and which exists for the purpose, in whole or in part, of dealing with employers concerning grievances, labor disputes, wages, rates of pay, hours, or other terms or conditions of employment, and any conference, general committee, joint or system board, or joint council so engaged which is subordinate to a national or international labor organization, other than a State or local central body.

(j) A labor organization shall be deemed to be engaged in an industry affecting commerce if it—

(1) is the certified representative of employees under the provisions of the National Labor Relations Act, as amended, or the Railway Labor Act, as amended; or

(2) although not certified, is a national or international labor organization or a local labor organization recognized or acting as the representative of employees of an employer or employers engaged in an industry affecting commerce; or

(3) has chartered a local labor organization or subsidiary body which is representing or actively seeking to represent employees of employers within the meaning of paragraph (1) or (2); or

(4) has been chartered by a labor organization representing or actively seeking to represent employees within the meaning of paragraph (1) or (2) as the local or subordinate body through which such employees may enjoy membership or become affiliated with such labor organization; or

(5) is a conference, general committee, joint or system board, or joint council, subordinate to a national or international labor organization, which includes a labor organization engaged in an industry affecting commerce within the meaning of any of the preceding paragraphs of this subsection, other than a State or local central body.

(k) "Secret ballot" means the expression by ballot, voting machine, or otherwise, but in no event by proxy, of a choice with respect to any election or vote taken upon any matter, which is cast in such a manner that the person expressing such choice cannot be identified with the choice expressed.

(*l*) "Trust in which a labor organization is interested" means a trust or other fund or organization (1) which was created or established by a labor organization, or one or more of the trustees or one or more members of the governing body of which is selected or appointed by a labor organization, and (2) a primary purpose of which is to provide benefits for the members of such labor organization or their beneficiaries.

(m) "Labor relations consultant" means any person who, for compensation, advises or represents an employer, employer organization, or labor organization concerning employee organizing, concerted activities, or collective bargaining activities.

(n) "Officer" means any constitutional officer, any person authorized to perform the functions of president, vice president, secretary, treasurer, or other executive functions of a labor organization, and any member of its executive board or similar governing body.

(o) "Member" or "member in good standing", when used in reference to a labor organization, includes any person who has fulfilled the requirements for membership in such organization, and who neither has voluntarily withdrawn from membership nor has been expelled or suspended from membership after appropriate proceedings consistent with lawful provisions of the constitution and bylaws of such organization.

(p) "Secretary" means the Secretary of Labor.

(q) "Officer, agent, shop steward, or other representative", when used with respect to a labor organization, includes elected officials and key administrative personnel, whether elected or appointed (such as business agents, heads of departments or major units, and organizers who exercise substantial independent authority), but does not include salaried nonsupervisory professional staff, stenographic, and service personnel.

(r) "District court of the United States" means a United States district court and a United States court of any place subject to the jurisdiction of the United States.

TITLE I. BILL OF RIGHTS OF MEMBERS OF LABOR ORGANIZATIONS

BILL OF RIGHTS

§ 101. (a)(1) *Equal Rights.*—Every member of a labor organization shall have equal rights and privileges within such organization to nominate candidates, to vote in elections or referendums of the labor organization, to attend membership meetings, and to participate in the deliberations and voting upon the business of such meetings, subject to reasonable rules and regulations in such organization's constitution and bylaws.

(2) *Freedom of Speech and Assembly.*—Every member of any labor organization shall have the right to meet and assemble freely with other members; and to express any views, arguments, or opinions; and to express at meetings of the labor organization his views, upon candidates in an election of the labor organization or upon any business properly before the meeting, subject to the organization's established and reasonable rules

pertaining to the conduct of meetings: *Provided*, That nothing herein shall be construed to impair the right of a labor organization to adopt and enforce reasonable rules as to the responsibility of every member toward the organization as an institution and to his refraining from conduct that would interfere with its performance of its legal or contractual obligations.

(3) *Dues, Initiation Fees, and Assessments.*—Except in the case of a federation of national or international labor organizations, the rates of dues and initiation fees payable by members of any labor organization in effect on the date of enactment of this Act shall not be increased, and no general or special assessment shall be levied upon such members, except—

(A) in the case of a local labor organization, (i) by majority vote by secret ballot of the members in good standing voting at a general or special membership meeting, after reasonable notice of the intention to vote upon such question, or (ii) by majority vote of the members in good standing voting in a membership referendum conducted by secret ballot; or

(B) in the case of a labor organization, other than a local labor organization or a federation of national or international labor organizations, (i) by majority vote of the delegates voting at a regular convention, or at a special convention of such labor organization held upon not less than thirty days' written notice to the principal office of each local or constituent labor organization entitled to such notice, or (ii) by majority vote of the members in good standing of such labor organization voting in a membership referendum conducted by secret ballot, or (iii) by majority vote of the members of the executive board or similar governing body of such labor organization, pursuant to express authority contained in the constitution and bylaws of such labor organization: Provided, That such action on the part of the executive board or similar governing body shall be effective only until the next regular convention of such labor organization.

(4) *Protection of the Right to Sue.*—No labor organization shall limit the right of any member thereof to institute an action in any court, or in a proceeding before any administrative agency, irrespective of whether or not the labor organization or its officers are named as defendants or respondents in such action or proceeding, or the right of any member of a labor organization to appear as a witness in any judicial, administrative, or legislative proceeding, or to petition any legislature or to communicate with any legislator: *Provided*, That any such member may be required to exhaust reasonable hearing procedures (but not to exceed a four-month lapse of time) within such organization, before instituting legal or administrative proceedings against such organizations or any officer thereof: *And provided further*, That no interested employer or employer association shall

directly or indirectly finance, encourage, or participate in, except as a party, any such action, proceeding, appearance, or petition.

(5) *Safeguards Against Improper Disciplinary Action.*—No member of any labor organization may be fined, suspended, expelled, or otherwise disciplined except for nonpayment of dues by such organization or by any officer thereof unless such member has been (A) served with written specific charges; (B) given a reasonable time to prepare his defense; (C) afforded a full and fair hearing.

(b) Any provision of the constitution and bylaws of any labor organization which is inconsistent with the provisions of this section shall be of no force or effect.

CIVIL ENFORCEMENT

§ 102. Any person whose rights secured by the provisions of this subchapter have been infringed by any violation of this subchapter may bring a civil action in a district court of the United States for such relief (including injunctions) as may be appropriate. Any such action against a labor organization shall be brought in the district court of the United States for the district where the alleged violation occurred, or where the principal office of such labor organization is located.

RETENTION OF EXISTING MEMBERS

§ 103. Nothing contained in this subchapter shall limit the rights and remedies of any member of a labor organization under any State or Federal law or before any court or other tribunal, or under the constitution and bylaws of any labor organization.

RIGHT TO COPIES OF COLLECTIVE BARGAINING AGREEMENTS

§ 104. It shall be the duty of the secretary or corresponding principal officer of each labor organization, in the case of a local labor organization, to forward a copy of each collective bargaining agreement made by such labor organization with any employer to any employee who requests such a copy and whose rights as such employee are directly affected by such agreement, and in the case of a labor organization other than a local labor organization, to forward a copy of any such agreement to each constituent unit which has members directly affected by such agreement; and such officer shall maintain at the principal office of the labor organization of which he is an officer copies of any such agreement made or received by such labor organization, which copies shall be available for inspection by any member or by any employee whose rights are affected by such agreement. The provisions of section 210 shall be applicable in the enforcement of this section.

INFORMATION AS TO ACT

§ 105. Every labor organization shall inform its members concerning the provisions of this Act.

Title II. Reporting by Labor Organizations, Officers and Employees of Labor Organizations, and Employers

REPORT OF LABOR ORGANIZATIONS

§ **201.** (a) Every labor organization shall adopt a constitution and bylaws and shall file a copy thereof with the Secretary, together with a report, signed by its president and secretary or corresponding principal officers, containing the following information—

(1) the name of the labor organization, its mailing address, and any other address at which it maintains its principal office or at which it keeps the records referred to in this title;

(2) the name and title of each of its officers;

(3) the initiation fee or fees required from a new or transferred member and fees for work permits required by the reporting labor organization;

(4) the regular dues or fees or other periodic payments required to remain a member of the reporting labor organization; and

(5) detailed statements, or references to specific provisions of documents filed under this subsection which contain such statements, showing the provision made and procedures followed with respect to each of the following: (A) qualifications for or restrictions on membership, (B) levying of assessments, (C) participation in insurance or other benefit plans, (D) authorization for disbursement of funds of the labor organization, (E) audit of financial transactions of the labor organization, (F) the calling of regular and special meetings, (G) the selection of officers and stewards and of any representatives to other bodies composed of labor organizations' representatives, with a specific statement of the manner in which each officer was elected, appointed, or otherwise selected, (H) discipline or removal of officers or agents for breaches of their trust, (I) imposition of fines, suspensions, and expulsions of members, including the grounds for such action and any provision made for notice, hearing, judgment on the evidence, and appeal procedures, (J) authorization for bargaining demands, (K) ratification of contract terms, (L) authorization for strikes, and (M) issuance of work permits. Any change in the information required by this subsection shall be reported to the Secretary at the time the reporting labor organization files with the Secretary the annual financial report required by subsection (b).

(b) Every labor organization shall file annually with the Secretary a financial report signed by its president and treasurer or corresponding principal officers containing the following information in such detail as may be necessary accurately to disclose its financial condition and operations for its preceding fiscal year—

(1) assets and liabilities at the beginning and end of the fiscal year;

(2) receipts of any kind and the sources thereof;

(3) salary, allowances, and other direct or indirect disbursements (including reimbursed expenses) to each officer and also to each employee who, during such fiscal year, received more than $10,000 in the aggregate from such labor organization and any other labor organization affiliated with it or with which it is affiliated, or which is affiliated with the same national or international labor organization;

(4) direct and indirect loans made to any officer, employee, or member, which aggregated more than $250 during the fiscal year, together with a statement of the purpose, security, if any, and arrangements for repayment;

(5) direct and indirect loans to any business enterprise, together with a statement of the purpose, security, if any, and arrangements for repayment; and

(6) other disbursements made by it including the purposes thereof; all in such categories as the Secretary may prescribe.

(c) Every labor organization required to submit a report under this title shall make available the information required to be contained in such report to all of its members, and every such labor organization and its officers shall be under a duty enforceable at the suit of any member of such organization in any State court of competent jurisdiction or in the district court of the United States for the district in which such labor organization maintains its principal office, to permit such member for just cause to examine any books, records, and accounts necessary to verify such report. The court in such action may, in its discretion, in addition to any judgment awarded to the plaintiff or plaintiffs, allow a reasonable attorney's fee to be paid by the defendant, and costs of the action.

REPORT OF OFFICERS AND EMPLOYEES OF LABOR ORGANIZATIONS

§ 202. (a) Every officer of a labor organization and every employee of a labor organization (other than an employee performing exclusively clerical or custodial services) shall file with the Secretary a signed report listing and describing for his preceding fiscal year—

(1) any stock, bond, security, or other interest, legal or equitable, which he or his spouse or minor child directly or indirectly held in, and any income or any other benefit with monetary value (including reimbursed expenses) which he or his spouse or minor child derived directly or indirectly from, an employer whose employees such labor organization represents or is actively seeking to represent, except payments and other benefits received as a bona fide employee of such employer;

(2) any transaction in which he or his spouse or minor child engaged, directly or indirectly, involving any stock, bond, security, or loan to or from, or other legal or equitable interest in the business of an employer whose employees such labor organization represents or is actively seeking to represent;

(3) any stock, bond, security, or other interest, legal or equitable, which he or his spouse or minor child directly or indirectly held in, and any income or any other benefit with monetary value (including reimbursed expenses) which he or his spouse or minor child directly or indirectly derived from, any business a substantial part of which consists of buying from, selling or leasing to, or otherwise dealing with, the business of an employer whose employees such labor organization represents or is actively seeking to represent;

(4) any stock, bond, security, or other interest, legal or equitable, which he or his spouse or minor child directly or indirectly held in, and any income or any other benefit with monetary value (including reimbursed expenses) which he or his spouse or minor child directly or indirectly derived from, a business any part of which consists of buying from, or selling or leasing directly or indirectly to, or otherwise dealing with such labor organization;

(5) any direct or indirect business transaction or arrangement between him or his spouse or minor child and any employer whose employees his organization represents or is actively seeking to represent, except work performed and payments and benefits received as a bona fide employee of such employer and except purchases and sales of goods or services in the regular course of business at prices generally available to any employee of such employer; and

(6) any payment of money or other thing of value (including reimbursed expenses) which he or his spouse or minor child received directly or indirectly from any employer or any person who acts as a labor relations consultant to an employer, except payments of the kinds referred to in section 302(c) of the Management Relations Act, 1947, as amended.

(b) The provisions of paragraphs (1), (2), (3), (4), and (5) of subsection (a) of this section shall not be construed to require any such officer or employee to report his bona fide investments in securities traded on a securities exchange registered as a national securities exchange under the Securities Exchange Act of 1934, in shares in an investment company registered under the Investment Company Act of 1940, or in securities of a public utility holding company registered under the Public Utility Holding Company Act of 1935, or to report any income derived therefrom.

(c) Nothing contained in this section shall be construed to require any officer or employee of a labor organization to file a report under subsection (a) unless he or his spouse or minor child holds or has held an interest, has received income or any other benefit with monetary value or a loan, or has engaged in a transaction described therein.

REPORT OF EMPLOYERS

§ **203.** (a) Every employer who in any fiscal year made—

(1) any payment or loan, direct or indirect, of money or other thing of value (including reimbursed expenses), or any promise or agreement there-

for, to any labor organization or officer, agent, shop steward, or other representative of a labor organization, or employee of any labor organization, except (A) payments or loans made by any national or State bank, credit union, insurance company, savings and loan association or other credit institution and (B) payments of the kind referred to in section 302(c) of the Labor Management Relations Act, 1947, as amended;

(2) any payment (including reimbursed expenses) to any of his employees, or any group or committee of such employees, for the purpose of causing such employee or group or committee of employees to persuade other employees to exercise or not to exercise, or as the manner of exercising, the right to organize and bargain collectively through representatives of their own choosing unless such payments were contemporaneously or previously disclosed to such other employees;

(3) any expenditure, during the fiscal year, where an object thereof, directly or indirectly, is to interfere with, restrain, or coerce employees in the exercise of the right to organize and bargain collectively through representatives of their own choosing, or is to obtain information concerning the activities of employees or a labor organization in connection with a labor dispute involving such employer, except for use solely in conjunction with an administrative or arbitral proceeding or a criminal or civil judicial proceeding;

(4) any agreement or arrangement with a labor relations consultant or other independent contractor or organization pursuant to which such person undertakes activities where an object thereof, directly or indirectly, is to persuade employees to exercise or not to exercise, or persuade employees as to the manner of exercising, the right to organize and bargain collectively through representatives of their own choosing, or undertakes to supply such employer with information concerning the activities of employees or a labor organization in connection with a labor dispute involving such employer, except information for use solely in conjunction with an administrative or arbitral proceeding or a criminal or civil judicial proceeding; or

(5) any payment (including reimbursed expenses) pursuant to an agreement or arrangement described in subdivision (4);

shall file with the Secretary a report, in a form prescribed by him, signed by its president and treasurer or corresponding principal officers showing in detail the date and amount of each such payment, loan, promise, agreement, or arrangement and the name, address, and position, if any, in any firm or labor organization of the person to whom it was made and a full explanation of the circumstances of all such payments, including the terms of any agreement or understanding pursuant to which they were made.

(b) Every person who pursuant to any agreement or arrangement with an employer undertakes activities where an object thereof is, directly or indirectly—

(1) to persuade employees to exercise or not to exercise, or persuade employees as to the manner of exercising, the right to organize and bargain collectively through representatives of their own choosing; or

(2) to supply an employer with information concerning the activities of employees or a labor organization in connection with a labor dispute involving such employer, except information for use solely in conjunction with an administrative or arbitral proceeding or a criminal or civil judicial proceeding;

shall file within thirty days after entering into such agreement or arrangement a report with the Secretary, signed by its president and treasurer or corresponding principal officers, containing the name under which such person is engaged in doing business and the address of its principal office, and a detailed statement of the terms and conditions of such agreement or arrangement. Every such person shall file annually, with respect to each fiscal year during which payments were made as a result of such an agreement or arrangement, a report with the Secretary, signed by its president and treasurer or corresponding principal officers, containing a statement (A) of its receipts of any kind from employers on account of labor relations advice or services, designating the sources thereof, and (B) of its disbursements of any kind, in connection with such services and the purposes thereof. In each such case such information shall be set forth in such categories as the Secretary may prescribe.

(c) Nothing in this section shall be construed to require any employer or other person to file a report covering the services of such person by reason of his giving or agreeing to give advice to such employer or representing or agreeing to represent such employer before any court, administrative agency, or tribunal of arbitration or engaging or agreeing to engage in collective bargaining on behalf of such employer with respect to wages, hours, or other terms or conditions of employment or the negotiation of an agreement or any question arising thereunder.

(d) Nothing contained in this section shall be construed to require an employer to file a report under subsection (a) of this section unless he has made an expenditure, payment, loan, agreement, or arrangement of the kind described therein. Nothing contained in this section shall be construed to require any other person to file a report under subsection (b) of this section unless he was a party to an agreement or arrangement of the kind described therein.

(e) Nothing contained in this section shall be construed to require any regular officer, supervisor, or employee of an employer to file a report in connection with services rendered to such employer nor shall any employer be required to file a report covering expenditures made to any regular officer, supervisor, or employee of an employer as compensation for service as a regular officer, supervisor, or employee of such employer.

(f) Nothing contained in this section shall be construed as an amendment to, or modification of the rights protected by, section 8(c) of the National Labor Relations Act, as amended.

(g) The term "interfere with, restrain, or coerce" as used in this section means interference, restraint, and coercion which, if done with respect to the exercise of rights guaranteed in section 7 of the National Labor Relations Act, as as amended, would, under section 8(a) of such Act, constitute an unfair labor practice. . . .

REPORTS MADE PUBLIC INFORMATION

§ 205. (a) The contents of the reports and documents filed with the Secretary pursuant to sections 201, 202, and 203 shall be public information, and the Secretary may publish any information and data which he obtains pursuant to the provisions of this title. The Secretary may use the information and data for statistical and research purposes, and compile and publish such studies, analyses, reports, and surveys based thereon as he may deem appropriate.

(b) The Secretary shall by regulation make reasonable provision for the inspection and examination, on the request of any person, of the information and data contained in any report or other document filed with him pursuant to sections 210, 202, or 203.

(c) The Secretary shall by regulation provide for the furnishing by the Department of Labor of copies of reports or other documents filed with the Secretary pursuant to this title, upon payment of a charge based upon the cost of the service. . . .

CRIMINAL PROVISIONS

§ 209. (a) Any person who willfully violates this title shall be fined not more than $10,000 or imprisoned for not more than one year, or both.

(b) Any person who makes a false statement or representation of a material fact, knowing it to be false, or who knowingly fails to disclose a material fact, in any document, report, or other information required under the provisions of this title shall be fined not more than $10,000 or imprisoned for not more than one year, or both.

(c) Any person who willfully makes a false entry in or willfully conceals, withholds, or destroys any books, records, reports, or statements required to be kept by any provision of this title shall be fined not more than $10,000 or imprisoned for not more than one year, or both.

(d) Each individual required to sign reports under sections 201 and 203 shall be personally responsible for the filing of such reports and for any statement contained therein which he knows to be false.

CIVIL ENFORCEMENT

§ 210. Whenever it shall appear that any person has violated or is about to violate any of the provisions of this title, the Secretary may bring a civil action for such relief (including injunctions) as may be appropriate. Any such action may be brought in the district court of the United States where the violation occurred or, at the option of the parties, in the United States District Court for the District of Columbia. . . .

TITLE III. TRUSTEESHIPS

REPORTS

§ 301. (a) Every labor organization which has or assumes trustee-ship over any subordinate labor organization shall file with the Secretary within thirty days after the date of the enactment of this Act or the imposition of any such trusteeship, and semiannually thereafter, a report, signed by its president and treasurer or corresponding principal officers, as well as by the trustees of such subordinate labor organization, containing the following information: (1) the name and address of the subordinate organization; (2) the date of establishing the trusteeship; (3) a detailed statement of the reason or reasons for establishing or continuing the trusteeship; and (4) the nature and extent of participation by the member-ship of the subordinate organization in the selection of delegates to repre-sent such organization in regular or special conventions or other policy-determining bodies and in the election of officers of the labor organization which has assumed trusteeship over such subordinate organization. The initial report shall also include a full and complete account of the financial condition of such subordinate organization as of the time trusteeship was assumed over it. During the continuance of a trusteeship the labor organization which has assumed trusteeship over a subordinate labor organization shall file on behalf of the subordinate labor organization the annual financial report required by section 201(b) signed by the president and treasurer or corresponding principal officers of the labor organization which has assumed such trusteeship and the trustees of the subordinate labor organization.

(b) The provisions of sections 201(c), 205, 206, 208, and 210 shall be applicable to reports filed under this title.

(c) Any person who willfully violates this section shall be fined not more than $10,000 or imprisoned for not more than one year, or both.

(d) Any person who makes a false statement or representation of a material fact, knowing it to be false, or who knowingly fails to disclose a material fact, in any report required under the provisions of this section or willfully makes any false entry in or willfully withholds, conceals, or destroys any documents, books, records, reports, or statements upon which such report is based, shall be fined not more than $10,000 or imprisoned for not more than one year, or both.

(e) Each individual required to sign a report under this section shall be personally responsible for the filing of such report and for any statement contained therein which he knows to be false.

PURPOSES FOR WHICH A TRUSTEESHIP MAY BE ESTABLISHED

§ 302. Trusteeships shall be established and administered by a labor organization over a subordinate body only in accordance with the constitution and bylaws of the organization which has assumed trusteeship over the subordinate body and for the purpose of correcting corruption or financial malpractice, assuring the performance of collective bargaining agreements or other duties of a bargaining representative, restoring democratic procedures, or otherwise carrying out the legitimate objects of such labor organization.

UNLAWFUL ACTS RELATING TO LABOR ORGANIZATION UNDER TRUSTEESHIP

§ 303. (a) During any period when a subordinate body of a labor organization is in trusteeship, it shall be unlawful (1) to count the vote of delegates from such body in any convention or election of officers of the labor organization unless the delegates have been chosen by secret ballot in an election in which all the members in good standing of such subordinate body were eligible to participate, or (2) to transfer to such organization any current receipts or other funds of the subordinate body except the normal per capita tax and assessments payable by subordinate bodies not in trusteeship: *Provided,* That nothing herein contained shall prevent the distribution of the assets of a labor organization in accordance with its constitution and bylaws upon the bona fide dissolution thereof.

(b) Any person who willfully violates this section shall be fined not more than $10,000 or imprisoned for not more than one year, or both.

ENFORCEMENT

§ 304. (a) Upon the written complaint of any member or subordinate body of a labor organization alleging that such organization has violated the provisions of this title (except section 301) the Secretary shall investigate the complaint and if the Secretary finds probable cause to believe that such violation has occurred and has not been remedied he shall, without disclosing the identity of the complainant, bring a civil action in any district court of the United States having jurisdiction of the labor organization for such relief (including injunctions) as may be appropriate. Any member or subordinate body of a labor organization affected by any violation of this title (except section 301) may bring a civil action in any district court of the United States having jurisdiction of the labor organization for such relief (including injunctions) as may be appropriate.

(b) For the purpose of actions under this section, district courts of the United States shall be deemed to have jurisdiction of a labor organization (1) in the district in which the principal office of such labor organization is located, or (2) in any district in which its duly authorized officers or agents are engaged in conducting the affairs of the trusteeship.

(c) In any proceeding pursuant to this section a trusteeship established by a labor organization in conformity with the procedural requirements of its constitution and bylaws and authorized or ratified after a fair hearing either before the executive board or before such other body as may be provided in accordance with its constitution or bylaws shall be presumed valid for a period of eighteen months from the date of its establishment and shall not be subject to attack during such period except upon clear and convincing proof that the trusteeship was not established or maintained in good faith for a purpose allowable under section 302. After the expiration of eighteen months the trusteeship shall be presumed invalid in any such proceeding and its discontinuance shall be decreed unless the labor organization shall show by clear and convincing proof that the continuation of the trusteeship is necessary for a purpose allowable under section 302. In the latter event the court may dismiss the complaint or retain jurisdiction of the cause on such conditions and for such period as it deems appropriate. . . .

COMPLAINT BY SECRETARY

§ 306. The rights and remedies provided by this title shall be in addition to any and all other rights and remedies at law or in equity: *Provided,* That upon the filing of a complaint by the Secretary the jurisdiction of the district court over such trusteeship shall be exclusive and the final judgment shall be res judicata.

TITLE IV. ELECTIONS

TERMS OF OFFICE; ELECTION PROCEDURES

§ 401. (a) Every national or international labor organization, except a federation of national or international labor organizations, shall elect its officers not less often than once every five years either by secret ballot among the members in good standing or at a convention of delegates chosen by secret ballot.

(b) Every local labor organization shall elect its officers not less often than once every three years by secret ballot among the members in good standing.

(c) Every national or international labor organization, except a federation of national or international labor organizations, and every local labor organization, and its officers, shall be under a duty, enforceable at the suit of any bona fide candidate for office in such labor organization in the district court of the United States in which such labor organization maintains its principal office, to comply with all reasonable requests of any candidate to distribute by mail or otherwise at the candidate's expense campaign literature in aid of such person's candidacy to all members in good standing of such labor organization and to refrain from discrimination in favor of or against any candidate with respect to the use of lists of members, and whenever such labor organizations or its officers authorize the distribution by mail or otherwise to members of campaign literature on behalf of any candidate or of the labor organization itself with reference to such election, similar distribution at the request of any other bona fide candidate shall be made by such labor organization and its officers, with equal treatment as to the expense of such distribution. Every bona fide candidate shall have the right, once within 30 days prior to an election of a labor organization in which he is a candidate, to inspect a list containing the names and last known addresses of all members of the labor organization who are subject to a collective bargaining agreement requiring membership therein as a condition of employment, which list shall be maintained and kept at the principal office of such labor organization by a designated official thereof. Adequate safeguards to insure a fair election shall be provided, including the right of any candidate to have an observer at the polls and at the counting of the ballots.

(d) Officers of intermediate bodies, such as general committees, system boards, joint boards, or joint councils, shall be elected not less often than once every four years by secret ballot among the members in good standing or by labor organization officers representative of such members who have been elected by secret ballot.

(e) In any election required by this section which is to be held by secret ballot a reasonable opportunity shall be given for the nomination of candidates and every member in good standing shall be eligible to be a candidate and to hold office (subject to section 504 and to reasonable qualifications uniformly imposed) and shall have the right to vote for or otherwise support the candidate or candidates of his choice, without being subject to penalty, discipline, or improper interference or reprisal of any kind by such organization or any member thereof. Not less than fifteen days prior to the election notice thereof shall be mailed to each member at his last known home address. Each member in good standing shall be entitled to one vote. No member whose dues have been withheld by his employer for payment to such organization pursuant to his voluntary authorization provided for in a collective bargaining agreement, shall be declared ineligible to vote or be a candidate for office in such organization by reason of alleged delay or default in the payment of dues. The votes cast by members of each local labor organization shall be counted, and the results published, separately. The election officials designated in the constitution and bylaws or the secretary, if no other official is designated, shall preserve for one year the ballots and all other records pertaining to the election. The election shall be conducted in accordance with the constitution and bylaws of such organization insofar as they are not inconsistent with the provisions of this title.

(f) When officers are chosen by a convention of delegates elected by secret ballot, the convention shall be conducted in accordance with the constitution and bylaws of the labor organization insofar as they are not inconsistent with the provisions of this title. The officials designated in the constitution and bylaws or the secretary, if no other is designated, shall preserve for one year the credentials of the delegates and all minutes and other records of the convention pertaining to the election of officers.

(g) No moneys received by any labor organization by way of dues, assessment, or similar levy, and no moneys of an employer shall be contributed or applied to promote the candidacy of any person in an election subject to the provisions of this title. Such moneys of a labor organization may be utilized for notices, factual statements of issues not involving candidates, and other expenses necessary for the holding of an election.

(h) If the Secretary, upon application of any member of a local labor organization, finds after hearing in accordance with the Administrative Procedure Act that the constitution and bylaws of such labor organization do not provide an adequate procedure for the removal of an elected officer guilty of serious misconduct, such officer may be removed, for cause shown and after notice and hearing, by the members in good standing voting in a secret ballot conducted by the officers of such labor organization in accordance with its constitution and bylaws insofar as they are not inconsistent with the provisions of this title.

(i) The Secretary shall promulgate rules and regulations prescribing minimum standards and procedures for determining the adequacy of the removal procedures to which reference is made in subsection (h).

ENFORCEMENT

§ 402. (a) A member of a labor organization—

(1) who has exhausted the remedies available under the constitution and bylaws of such organization and of any parent body or

(2) who has invoked such available remedies without obtaining a final decision within three calendar months after their invocation,

may file a complaint with the Secretary within one calendar month thereafter alleging the violation of any provision of section 401 (including violation of the constitution and bylaws of the labor organization pertaining to the election and removal of officers). The challenged election shall be presumed valid pending a final decision thereon (as hereinafter provided) and in the interim the affairs of the organization shall be conducted by the officers elected or in such other manner as its constitution and bylaws may provide.

(b) The Secretary shall investigate such complaint and, if he finds probable cause to believe that a violation of this title has occurred and has not been remedied, he shall, within sixty days after the filing of such complaint, bring a civil action against the labor organization as an entity in the district court of the United States in which such labor organization maintains its principal office to set aside the invalid election, if any, and to direct the conduct of an election or hearing and vote upon the removal of officers under the supervision of the Secretary and in accordance with the provisions of this title and such rules and regulations as the Secretary may prescribe. The court shall have power to take such action as it deems proper to preserve the assets of the labor organization.

(c) If, upon a preponderance of the evidence after a trial upon the merits, the court finds—

(1) that an election has not been held within the time prescribed by section 401, or

(2) that the violation of section 401 may have affected the outcome of an election,

that court shall declare the election, if any, to be void and direct the conduct of a new election under supervision of the Secretary and, so far as lawful and practicable, in conformity with the constitution and bylaws of the labor organization. The Secretary shall promptly certify to the court the names of the persons elected, and the court shall thereupon enter a decree declaring such persons to be the officers of the labor organization. If the proceeding is for the removal of officers pursuant to subsection (h) of section 401, the Secretary shall certify the results of the vote and the court shall enter a decree declaring whether such persons have been removed as officers of the labor organization.

(d) An order directing an election, dismissing a complaint, or designating elected officers of a labor organization shall be appealable in the same manner as the final judgment in a civil action, but an order directing an election shall not be stayed pending appeal.

APPLICATION OF OTHER LAWS

§ 403. No labor organization shall be required by law to conduct elections of officers with greater frequency or in a different form or manner than is required by its own constitution or bylaws, except as otherwise provided by this title. Existing rights and remedies to enforce the constitution and bylaws of a labor organization with respect to elections prior to the conduct thereof shall not be affected by the provisions of this title. The remedy provided by this title for challenging an election already conducted shall be exclusive....

TITLE V. SAFEGUARDS FOR LABOR ORGANIZATIONS

FIDUCIARY RESPONSIBILITY OF OFFICERS OF LABOR ORGANIZATIONS

§ 501. (a) The officers, agents, shop stewards, and other representatives of a labor organization occupy positions of trust in relation to such organization and its members as a group. It is, therefore, the duty of each such person, taking into account the special problems and functions of a labor organization, to hold its money and property solely for the benefit of the organization and its members and to manage, invest, and expend the same in accordance with its constitution and bylaws and any resolutions of the governing bodies adopted thereunder, to refrain from dealing with such organization as an adverse party or in behalf of an adverse party in any matter connected with his duties and from holding or acquiring any pecuniary or personal interest which conflicts with the interests of such organization, and to account to the organization for any profit received by him in whatever capacity in connection with transactions conducted by him or under his direction on behalf of the organization. A general exculpatory provision in the constitution and bylaws of such a labor organization or a general exculpatory resolution of a governing body purporting to relieve any such person of liability for breach of the duties declared by this section shall be void as against public policy.

(b) When any officer, agent, shop steward, or representative of any labor organization is alleged to have violated the duties declared in subsection (a) of this section and the labor organization or its governing board or officers refuse or fail to sue or recover damages or secure an accounting or other appropriate relief within a reasonable time after being requested to do so by any member of the labor organization, such member may sue such officer, agent, shop steward, or representative in any district court of the United States or in any State court of competent jurisdiction to recover damages or secure an accounting or other appropriate relief for the benefit of the labor organization. No such proceeding shall be brought except upon leave of the court obtained upon verified application and for good cause shown, which application may be made ex parte. The trial judge may allot a reasonable part of the recovery in any action under this subsection to pay the fees of counsel prosecuting the suit at the instance of the member of the labor organization and to compensate such member for any expenses necessarily paid or incurred by him in connection with the litigation.

(c) Any person who embezzles, steals, or unlawfully and willfully abstracts or converts to his own use, or the use of another, any of the moneys, funds, securities, property, or other assets of a labor organization of which he is an officer, or by which he is employed, directly or indirectly, shall be fined not more than $10,000 or imprisoned for not more than five years, or both.

BONDING*

§ **502.** (a) Every officer, agent, shop steward, or other representative or employee of any labor organization (other than a labor organization whose property and annual financial receipts do not exceed $5,000 in value), or of a trust in which a labor organization is interested, who handles funds or other property thereof shall be bonded |for te faithful discharge of his duties] to provide protection against loss by reason of acts

* As amended, Pub. L. 89-216, § 1, Sept. 29, 1965, 79 stat. 888. Omitted language is in   brackets, new language is underscored—ED.

of fraud or dishonesty on his part directly or through connivance with others. The bond of each such person shall be fixed at the beginning of the organization's fiscal year and shall be in an amount not less than 10 per centum of the funds handled by him and his predecessor or predecessors, if any, during the preceding fiscal year, but in no case more than $500,000. If the labor organization or the trust in which a labor organization is interested does not have a preceding fiscal year, the amount of the bond shall be, in the case of a local labor organization, not less than $1,000, and in the case of any other labor organization or of a trust in which a labor organization is interested, not less than $10,000. Such bonds shall be individual or schedule in form, and shall have a corporate surety company as surety thereon. Any person who is not covered by such bonds shall not be permitted to receive, handle, disburse, or otherwise exercise custody or control of the funds or other property of a labor organization or of a trust in which a labor organization is interested. No such bond shall be placed through an agent or broker or with a surety company in which any labor organization or any officer, agent, shop steward, or other representative of a labor organization has any direct or indirect interest. Such surety company shall be a corporate surety which holds a grant of authority from the Secretary of the Treasury the Act of July 30, 1947 (6 U.S.C. 6 to 13), as an acceptable surety on Federal bonds: *Provided*, That when in the opinion of the Secretary a labor organization has made other bonding arrangements which would provide the protection required by this section at comparable cost or less, he may exempt such labor organization from placing a bond through a surety company holding such grant of authority.

(b) Any person who willfully violates this section shall be fined not more than $10,000 or imprisoned for not more than one year, or both.

MAKING OF LOANS; PAYMENT OF FINES

§ 503. (a) No labor organization shall make directly or indirectly any loan or loans to any officer or employee of such organization which results in a total indebtedness on the part of such officer or employee to the labor organization in excess of $2,000.

(b) No labor organization or employer shall directly or indirectly pay the fine of any officer or employee convicted of any willful violation of this Act.

(c) Any person who willfully violates this section shall be fined not more than $5,000 or imprisoned for not more than one year, or both.

PROHIBITION AGAINST CERTAIN PERSONS HOLDING OFFICE

§ 504.* (a)No person who is or has been a member of the Communist Party or who has been convicted of, or served any part of a prison term

---

* This section reflects amendments made   2133 (1984).—Ed.
by Pub.L. 98-473, Title II, § 803, 98 Stat.

resulting from his conviction of, robbery, bribery, extortion, embezzlement, grand larceny, burglary, arson, violation of narcotics laws, murder, rape, assault with intent to kill, assault which inflicts grievous bodily injury, or a violation of subchapter III or IV of this chapter any felony involving abuse or misuse of such person's position or employment in a labor organization or employee benefit plan to seek or obtain an illegal gain at the expense of the members of the labor organization or the beneficiaries of the employee benefit plan, or conspiracy to commit any such crimes or attempt to commit any such crimes, or a crime in which any of the foregoing crimes is an element, shall serve or be permitted to serve—

(1) as a consultant or adviser to any labor organization,

(2) as an officer, director, trustee, member of any executive board or similar governing body, business agent, manager, organizer, employee, or representative in any capacity of any labor organization,

(3) as a labor relations consultant or adviser to a person engaged in an industry or activity affecting commerce, or as an officer, director, agent, or employee of any group or association of employers dealing with any labor organization, or in a position having specific collective bargaining authority or direct responsibility in the area of labor-management relations in any corporation or association engaged in an industry or activity affecting commerce, or

(4) in a position which entitles its occupant to a share of the proceeds of, or as an officer or executive or administrative employee of, any entity whose activities are in whole or substantial part devoted to providing goods or services to any labor organization, or

(5) in any capacity, other than in his capacity as a member of such labor organization, that involves decisionmaking authority concerning, or decisionmaking authority over, or custody of, or control of the moneys, funds, assets, or property of any labor organization,

during or for the period of thirteen years after such conviction or after the end of such imprisonment, whichever is later, unless the sentencing court on the motion of the person convicted sets a lesser period of at least three years after such conviction or after the end of such imprisonment, whichever is later, or unless prior to the end of such period, in the case of a person so convicted or imprisoned, (A) his citizenship rights, having been revoked as a result of such conviction, have been fully restored, or (B) if the offense is a Federal offense, the sentencing judge or, if the offense is a State or local offense, the United States district court for the district in which the offense was committed, pursuant to sentencing guidelines and policy statements under section 994(a) of Title 28, determines that such person's service in any capacity referred to in clauses (1) through (5) would not be contrary to the purposes of this chapter. Prior to making any such determination the Commission shall hold a hearing and shall give notice of such proceeding by certified mail to the Secretary of Labor and to State, county, and Federal prosecuting officials in the jurisdiction or jurisdictions in which such person was convicted. The Commission's determination in any such proceeding shall be final. No person shall knowingly hire, retain, employ, or otherwise place any other person to serve in any capacity in violation of this subsection.

(b) Any person who willfully violates this section shall be fined not more than $10,000 or imprisoned for not more than five years, or both.

(c) For the purpose of this section—

(1) A person shall be deemed to have been "convicted" and under the disability of "conviction" from the date of the judgment of the trial court, regardless of whether that judgment remains under appeal.

(2) A period of parole shall not be considered as part of a period of imprisonment.

(d) Whenever any person—

(1) by operation of this section, has been barred from office or other position in a labor organization as a result of a conviction, and

(2) has filed an appeal of that conviction,

any salary which would be otherwise due such person by virtue of such office or position, shall be placed in escrow by the individual employer or organization responsible for payment of such salary. Payment of such salary into escrow shall continue for the duration of the appeal or for the period of time during which such salary would be otherwise due, whichever period is shorter. Upon the final reversal of such person's conviction on appeal, the amounts in escrow shall be paid to such person. Upon the final sustaining of such person's conviction on appeal, the amounts in escrow shall be returned to the individual employer or organization responsible for payments of those amounts. Upon final reversal of such person's conviction, such person shall no longer be barred by this statute from assuming any position from which such person was previously barred.

TITLE VI. MISCELLANEOUS PROVISIONS

INVESTIGATIONS

§ 601. (a) The Secretary shall have power when he believes it necessary in order to determine whether any person has violated or is about to violate any provision of this Act (except title I or amendments made by this Act to other statutes) to make an investigation and in connection therewith he may enter such places and inspect such records and accounts and question such persons as he may deem necessary to enable him to determine the facts relative thereto. The Secretary may report to interested persons or officials concerning the facts required to be shown in any report required by this Act and concerning the reasons for failure or refusal to file such a report or any other matter which he deems to be appropriate as a result of such an investigation. . . .

EXTORTIONATE PICKETING

§ 602. (a) It shall be unlawful to carry on picketing on or about the premises of any employer for the purpose of, or as part of any conspiracy or in furtherance of any plan or purpose for, the personal profit or enrichment of any individual (except a bona fide increase in wages or other employee benefits) by taking or obtaining any money or other thing of value from such employer against his will or with his consent.

(b) Any person who willfully violates this section shall be fined not more than $10,000 or imprisoned not more than twenty years, or both.

RETENTION OF RIGHTS UNDER OTHER FEDERAL AND STATE LAWS

§ 603. (a) Except as explicitly provided to the contrary, nothing in this Act shall reduce or limit the responsibilities of any labor organization or any officer, agent, shop steward, or other representative of a labor organization, or of any trust in which a labor organization is interested, under any other Federal law or under the laws of any State, and, except as explicitly provided to the contrary, nothing in this Act shall take away any right or bar any remedy to which members of a labor organization are entitled under such other Federal law or law of any State.

(b) Nothing contained in titles I, II, III, IV, V, or VI of this Act shall be construed to supersede or impair or otherwise affect the provisions of the Railway Labor Act, as amended, or any of the obligations, rights, benefits, privileges, or immunities of any carrier, employee, organization, representative, or person subject thereto; nor shall anything contained in said titles (except section 505) of this Act be construed to confer any rights, privileges, immunities, or defenses upon employers, or to impair or otherwise affect the rights of any person under the National Labor Relations Act, as amended.

EFFECT ON STATE LAWS

§ 604. Nothing in this Act shall be construed to impair or diminish the authority of any State to enact and enforce general criminal laws with respect to robbery, bribery, extortion, embezzlement, grand larceny, burglary, arson, violation of narcotics laws, murder, rape, assault with intent to kill, or assault which inflicts grievous bodily injury, or conspiracy to commit any of such crimes. . . .

PROHIBITION ON CERTAIN DISCIPLINE BY LABOR ORGANIZATION

§ 609. It shall be unlawful for any labor organization, or any officer, agent, shop steward, or other representative of a labor organization, or any employee thereof to fine, suspend, expel, or otherwise discipline any of its members for exercising any right to which he is entitled under the provisions of this Act. The provisions of section 102 shall be applicable in the enforcement of this section.

DEPRIVATION OF RIGHTS UNDER ACT BY VIOLENCE

§ 610.   It shall be unlawful for any person through the use of force or violence, to restrain, coerce, or intimidate, or attempt to restrain, coerce, or intimidate any member of a labor organization for the purpose of interfering with or preventing the exercise of any right to which he is entitled under the provisions of this Act.   Any person who willfully violates this section shall be fined not more than $1,000 or imprisoned for not more than one year, or both.

SEPARABILITY PROVISIONS

§ 611.   If any provision of this Act, or the application of such provision to any person or circumstances, shall be held invalid, the remainder of this Act or the application of such provision to persons or circumstances other than those as to which it is held invalid, shall not be affected thereby.

FEDERAL ARBITRATION ACT

61 Stat. 669 (1947), as amended (derived from
43 Stat. 883 (1925)); 9 U.S.C. §§ 1–16

§ 1. "Maritime Transactions" and "Commerce" Defined; Exceptions to Operation of Title

"Maritime transactions", as herein defined, means charter parties, bills of lading of water carriers, agreements relating to wharfage, supplies furnished vessels or repairs to vessels, collisions, or any other matters in foreign commerce which, if the subject of controversy, would be embraced within admiralty jurisdiction; "commerce", as herein defined, means commerce among the several States or with foreign nations, or in any Territory of the United States or in the District of Columbia, or between any such Territory and another, or between any such Territory and any State or foreign nation, or between the District of Columbia and any State or Territory or foreign nation, but nothing herein contained shall apply to contracts of employment of seamen, railroad employees, or any other class of workers engaged in foreign or interstate commerce.

§ 2. Validity, Irrevocability and Enforcement of Agreements to Arbitrate

A written provision in any maritime transaction or a contract evidencing a transaction involving commerce to settle by arbitration a controversy thereafter arising out of such contract or transaction, or the refusal to perform the whole or any part thereof, or an agreement in writing to submit to arbitration an existing controversy arising out of such a contract, transaction, or refusal, shall be valid, irrevocable, and enforceable, save upon such grounds as exist at law or in equity for the revocation of any contract.

§ 3. Stay of Proceedings Where Issue Therein Referable to Arbitration

If any suit or proceeding be brought in any of the courts of the United States upon any issue referable to arbitration under an agreement in writing for such arbitration, the court in which such suit is pending, upon being satisfied that the issue involved in such suit or proceeding is referable to arbitration under such an agreement, shall on application of one of the parties stay the trial of the action until such arbitration has been had in accordance with the terms of the agreement, providing the applicant for the stay is not in default in proceeding with such arbitration.

§ 4.   Failure to Arbitrate Under Agreement; Petition to United States Court Having Jurisdiction for Order to Compel Arbitration; Notice and Service Thereof; Hearing and Determination

A party aggrieved by the alleged failure, neglect, or refusal of another to arbitrate under a written agreement for arbitration may petition any United States district court which, save for such agreement, would have jurisdiction under Title 28, in a civil action or in admiralty of the subject matter of a suit arising out of the controversy between the parties, for an order directing that such arbitration proceed in the manner provided for in such agreement. Five days' notice in writing of such application shall be served upon the party in default. Service thereof shall be made in the manner provided by the Federal Rules of Civil Procedure. The court shall hear the parties, and upon being satisfied that the making of the agreement for arbitration or the failure to comply therewith is not in issue, the court shall make an order directing the parties to proceed to arbitration in accordance with the terms of the agreement. The hearing and proceedings, under such agreement, shall be within the district in which the petition for an order directing such arbitration is filed. If the making of the arbitration agreement or the failure, neglect, or refusal to perform the same be in issue, the court shall proceed summarily to the trial thereof. If no jury trial be demanded by the party alleged to be in default, or if the matter in dispute is within admiralty jurisdiction, the court shall hear and determine such issue. Where such an issue is raised, the party alleged to be in default may, except in cases of admiralty, on or before the return day of the notice of application, demand a jury trial of such issue, and upon such demand the court shall make an order referring the issue or issues to a jury in the manner provided by the Federal Rules of Civil Procedure, or may specially call a jury for that purpose. If the jury find that no agreement in writing for arbitration was made or that there is no default in proceeding thereunder, the proceeding shall be dismissed. If the jury find that an agreement for arbitration was made in writing and that there is a default in proceeding thereunder, the court shall make an order summarily directing the parties to proceed with the arbitration in accordance with the terms thereof.

§ 5.   Appointment of Arbitrators or Umpire

If in the agreement provision be made for a method of naming or appointing an arbitrator or arbitrators or an umpire, such method shall be followed; but if no method be provided therein, or if a method be provided and any party thereto shall fail to avail himself of such method, or if for any other reason there shall be a lapse in the naming of an arbitrator or arbitrators or umpire, or in filling a vacancy, then upon the application of either party to the controversy the court shall designate and appoint an arbitrator or arbitrators or umpire, as the case may require, who shall act under the said agreement with the same force and effect as if he or they had been specifically named therein; and unless otherwise provided in the agreement the arbitration shall be by a single arbitrator.

§ 6. Application Heard as Motion

Any application to the court hereunder shall be made and heard in the manner provided by law for the making and hearing of motions, except as otherwise herein expressly provided.

§ 7. Witnesses Before Arbitrators; Fees; Compelling Attendance

The arbitrators selected either as prescribed in this title or otherwise, or a majority of them, may summon in writing any person to attend before them or any of them as a witness and in a proper case to bring with him or them any book, record, document, or paper which may be deemed material as evidence in the case. The fees for such attendance shall be the same as the fees of witnesses before masters of the United States courts. Said summons shall issue in the name of the arbitrator or arbitrators, or a majority of them, and shall be signed by the arbitrators, or a majority of them, and shall be directed to the said person and shall be served in the same manner as subpoenas to appear and testify before the court; if any person or persons so summoned to testify shall refuse or neglect to obey said summons, upon petition the United States district court for the district in which such arbitrators, or a majority of them, are sitting may compel the attendance of such person or persons before said arbitrator or arbitrators, or punish said person or persons for contempt in the same manner provided by law for securing the attendance of witnesses or their punishment for neglect or refusal to attend in the courts of the United States.

§ 8. Proceedings Begun by Libel in Admiralty and Seizure of Vessel or Property

If the basis of jurisdiction be a cause of action otherwise justiciable in admiralty, then, notwithstanding anything herein to the contrary, the party claiming to be aggrieved may begin his proceeding hereunder by libel and seizure of the vessel or other property of the other party according to the usual course of admiralty proceedings, and the court shall then have jurisdiction to direct the parties to proceed with the arbitration and shall retain jurisdiction to enter its decree upon the award.

§ 9. Award of Arbitrators; Confirmation; Jurisdiction; Procedure

If the parties in their agreement have agreed that a judgment of the court shall be entered upon the award made pursuant to the arbitration, and shall specify the court, then at any time within one year after the award is made any party to the arbitration may apply to the court so specified for an order confirming the award, and thereupon the court must grant such an order unless the award is vacated, modified, or corrected as prescribed in sections 10 and 11 of this title. If no court is specified in the agreement of the parties, then such application may be made to the United States court in and for the district within which such award was made. Notice of the application shall be served upon the adverse party, and thereupon the court shall have jurisdiction of such party as though he had appeared generally in the proceeding. If the adverse party is a resident of the district within which the award was made, such service shall be made upon the adverse party or his attorney as prescribed by law for service of notice of motion in an action in the same court. If the adverse party shall be a nonresident, then the notice of the application shall be served by the marshal of any district within which the adverse party may be found in like manner as other process of the court.

§ 10. Same; Vacation; Grounds; Rehearing

(a) In any of the following cases the United States court in and for the district wherein the award was made may make an order vacating the award upon the application of any party to the arbitration—

(1) Where the award was procured by corruption, fraud, or undue means.

(2) Where there was evident partiality or corruption in the arbitrators, or either of them.

(3) Where the arbitrators were guilty of misconduct in refusing to postpone the hearing, upon sufficient cause shown, or in refusing to hear evidence pertinent and material to the controversy; or of any other misbehavior by which the rights of any party have been prejudiced.

(4) Where the arbitrators exceeded their powers, or so imperfectly executed them that a mutual, final, and definite award upon the subject matter submitted was not made.

(5) Where an award is vacated and the time within which the agreement required the award to be made has not expired the court may, in its discretion, direct a rehearing by the arbitrators.

(b) The United States district court for the district wherein an award was made that was issued pursuant to section 580 of title 5 may make an order vacating the award upon the application of a person, other than a party to the arbitration, who is adversely affected or aggrieved by the award, if the use of arbitration or the award is clearly inconsistent with the factors set forth in section 572 of title 5.

§ 11. Same; Modification or Correction; Grounds; Order

In either of the following cases the United States court in and for the district wherein the award was made may make an order modifying or correcting the award upon the application of any party to the arbitration—

(a) Where there was an evident material miscalculation of figures or an evident material mistake in the description of any person, thing, or property referred to in the award.

(b) Where the arbitrators have awarded upon a matter not submitted to them, unless it is a matter not affecting the merits of the decision upon the matter submitted.

(c) Where the award is imperfect in matter of form not affecting the merits of the controversy.

The order may modify and correct the award, so as to effect the intent thereof and promote justice between the parties.

§ 12. Notice of motions to vacate or modify; service; stay of proceedings

Notice of a motion to vacate, modify, or correct an award must be served upon the adverse party or his attorney within three months after the award is filed or delivered. If the adverse party is a resident of the district within which the award was made, such service shall be made upon the adverse party or his attorney as prescribed by law for service of notice of motion in an action in the same court. If the adverse party shall be a nonresident then the notice of the application shall be served by the marshal of any district within which the adverse party may be found in like manner as other process of the court. For the purposes of the motion any judge who might make an order to stay the proceedings in an action brought in the same court may make an order, to be served with the notice of motion, staying the proceedings of the adverse party to enforce the award.

§ 13. Papers Filed With Order on Motions; Judgment; Docketing; Force and Effect; Enforcement

The party moving for an order confirming, modifying, or correcting an award shall, at the time such order is filed with the clerk for the entry of judgment thereon, also file the following papers with the clerk:

(a) The agreement; the selection or appointment, if any, of an additional arbitrator or umpire; and each written extension of the time, if any, within which to make the award.

(b) The award.

(c) Each notice, affidavit, or other paper used upon an application to confirm, modify, or correct the award, and a copy of each order of the court upon such an application.

The judgment shall be docketed as if it was rendered in an action.

The judgment so entered shall have the same force and effect, in all respects, as, and be subject to all the provisions of law relating to, a judgment in an action; and it may be enforced as if it had been rendered in an action in the court in which it is entered.

§ 14. Contracts Not Affected

This title shall not apply to contracts made prior to January 1, 1926.

§ 15. Inapplicability of the Act of State doctrine

Enforcement of arbitral agreements, confirmation of arbitral awards, and execution upon judgments based on orders confirming such awards shall not be refused on the basis of the Act of State doctrine.

§ 16. Appeals

(a) An appeal may be taken from—

(1) an order—

(A) refusing a stay of any action under section 3 of this title,

(B) denying a petition under section 4 of this title to order arbitration to proceed,

(C) denying an application under section 206 of this title to compel arbitration,

(D) confirming or denying confirmation of an award or partial award, or

(E) modifying, correcting, or vacating an award;

(2) an interlocutory order granting, continuing, or modifying an injunction against an arbitration that is subject to this title; or

(3) a final decision with respect to an arbitration that is subject to this title.

(b) Except as otherwise provided in section 1292(b) of title 28, an appeal may not be taken from an interlocutory order—

(1) granting a stay of any action under section 3 of this title;

(2) directing arbitration to proceed under section 4 of this title;

(3) compelling arbitration under section 206 of this title; or

(4) refusing to enjoin an arbitration that is subject to this title.

MODEL EMPLOYMENT TERMINATION ACT

National Conference of Commissioners on Uniform State Laws 1991

[Editor's Note: Brackets indicate possible deletions or alternatives for particular state legislatures to consider.]

§ 1. Definitions.

In this [Act]:

(1) "Employee" means an individual who works for hire, including an individual employed in a supervisory, managerial, or confidential position, but not an independent contractor.

(2) "Employer" means a person [, excluding this State, a political subdivision, a municipal corporation, or any other governmental subdivision, agency, or instrumentality,] that has employed [five] or more employees for each working day in each of 20 or more calendar weeks in the two-year period next preceding a termination or an employer's filing of a complaint pursuant to Section 5(c), excluding a parent, spouse, child, or other member of the employer's immediate family or of the immediate family of an individual having a controlling interest in the employer.

(3) "Fringe benefit" means vacation leave, sick leave, medical insurance plan, disability insurance plan, life insurance plan, pension benefit plan, or other benefit of economic value, to the extent the leave, plan, or benefit is paid for by the employer.

(4) "Good cause" means (i) a reasonable basis related to an individual employee for termination of the employee's employment in view of relevant factors and circumstances, which may include the employee's duties, responsibilities, conduct on the job or otherwise, job performance, and employment record, or (ii) the exercise of business judgment in good faith by the employer, including setting its economic or institutional goals and determining methods to achieve those goals, organizing or reorganizing operations, discontinuing, consolidating, or divesting operations or positions or parts of operations or positions, determining the size of its work force and the nature of the positions filled by its work force, and determining and changing standards of performance for positions.

(5) "Good faith" means honesty in fact.

(6) "Pay," as a noun, means hourly wages or periodic salary, including tips, regularly paid and nondiscretionary commissions and bonuses, and regularly paid overtime, but not fringe benefits.

(7) "Person" means an individual, corporation, business trust, estate, trust, partnership, association, joint venture, or any other legal or commercial entity [, excluding government or a governmental subdivision, agency, or instrumentality].

(8) "Termination" means:

(i) a dismissal, including that resulting from the elimination of a position, of an employee by an employer;

(ii) a layoff or suspension of an employee by an employer for more than two consecutive months; or

(iii) a quitting of employment or a retirement by an employee induced by an act or omission of the employer, after notice to the employer of the act or omission without appropriate relief by the employer, so intolerable that under the circumstances a reasonable individual would quit or retire.

§ 2. Scope.

(a) This [Act] applies only to a termination that occurs after the effective date of this [Act].

(b) This [Act] does not apply to a termination at the expiration of an express oral or written agreement of employment for a specified duration, which was valid, subsisting, and in effect on the [effective] date of this [Act].

(c) Except as provided in subsection (e), this [Act] displaces and extinguishes all common-law rights and claims of a terminated employee against the employer, its officers, directors, and employees, which are based on the termination or on acts taken or statements made that are reasonably necessary to initiate or effect the termination if the employee's termination requires good cause under Section 3(a), is subject to an agreement for severance pay under Section 4(c), or is permitted by the expiration of an agreement for a specified duration under Section 4(d).

(d) An employee whose termination is not subject to Section 3(a) or 4(d) and who is not a party to an agreement under Section 4(c) retains all common-law rights and claims.

(e) This [Act] does not displace or extinguish rights or claims of a terminated employee against an employer arising under state or federal statutes or administrative rules or regulations having the force of law [or local ordinances valid under state law], a collective-bargaining agreement between an employer and a labor organization, or an express oral or written agreement relating to employment which does not violate this [Act]. Those rights and claims may not be asserted under this [Act], except as otherwise provided in this [Act]. The existence or adjudication of those rights or claims does not limit the employee's rights or claims under this [Act], except as stated in Section 7(d).

§ 3. Prohibited Terminations.

(a) Unless otherwise provided in an agreement for severance pay under Section 4(c) or for a specified duration under Section 4(d), an employer may not terminate the employment of an employee without good cause.

(b) Subsection (a) applies only to an employee who has been employed by the same employer for a total period of one year or more and has worked for the employer for at least 520 hours during the 26 weeks next preceding the termination. A layoff or other break in service is not counted in determining whether an employee's period of employment totals one year, but the employee is considered to be employed during paid vacations and other authorized leaves. If an employee is rehired after a break in service exceeding one year, not counting absences due to labor disputes or authorized leaves, the employee is considered to be newly hired. The 26–week period for purposes of this subsection does not include any week during which the employee was absent because of layoffs of one year or less, paid vacations, authorized leaves, or labor disputes.

§ 4. Agreements Between Employer and Employee.

(a) A right of an employee under this [Act] may not be waived by agreement except as provided in this section.

(b) By express written agreement, an employer and an employee may provide that the employee's failure to meet specified business-related standards of performance or the employee's commission or omission of specified business-related acts will constitute good cause for termination in proceedings under this [Act]. Those standards or prohibitions are effective only if they have been consistently enforced and they have not been applied to a particular employee in a disparate manner without justification. If the agreement authorizes changes by the employer in the standards or prohibitions, the changes must be clearly communicated to the employee.

(c) By express written agreement, an employer and an employee may mutually waive the requirement of good cause for termination, if the employer agrees that upon the termination of the employee for any reason other than willful misconduct of the employee, the employer will provide severance pay in an amount equal to at least one month's pay for each period of employment totaling one year, up to a maximum total payment equal to 30 months' pay at the employee's rate of pay in effect immediately before the termination. The employer shall make the payment in a lump sum or in a series of monthly installments, none of which may be less than one month's pay plus interest on the principal balance. The lump-sum payment must be made or payment of the monthly installments must begin within 30 days after the employee's termination. An agreement under this subsection constitutes a waiver by the employer and the employee of the right to civil trial, including jury trial, concerning disputes over the nature of the termination and the employee's entitlement to severance pay, and constitutes a stipulation by the parties that those disputes will be subject to the procedures and remedies of this [Act].

(d) The requirement of good cause for termination does not apply to the termination of an employee at the expiration of an express oral or written agreement of employment for a specified duration related to the completion of a specified task, project, undertaking, or assignment. If the employment continues after the expiration of the agreement, Section 3 applies to its termination unless the parties enter into a new express oral or written agreement under this subsection. The period of employment under an agreement described in this subsection counts toward the minimum periods of employment required by Section 3(b).

(e) An employer may provide substantive and procedural rights in addition to those provided by this [Act], either to one or more specific employees by express oral or written agreement, or to employees generally by a written personnel policy or statement, and may provide that those rights are enforceable under the procedures of this [Act].

(f) An employing person and an employee not otherwise subject to this [Act] may become subject to its provisions to the extent provided by express written agreement, in which case the employing person is deemed to be an employer.

(g) An agreement between an employer and an employee subject to this [Act] imposes a duty of good faith in its formation, performance, and enforcement.

(h) By express written agreement, an employer and an employee may settle at any time a claim arising under this [Act].

(i) By express written agreement before or after a dispute or claim arises under this [Act], an employer and an employee may agree to private arbitration or other alternative dispute-resolution procedure for resolving the dispute or claim.

(j) By express written agreement after a dispute or claim arises under this [Act], an employer and an employee may agree to judicial resolution of the dispute or claim.

(k) The substantive provisions of this [Act] apply under an agreement authorized by subsections (i) and (j).

§ 5. Procedure and Limitations.

(a) An employee whose employment is terminated may file a complaint and demand for arbitration under this [Act] with the [Commission; Department; Service] not later than 180 days after the effective date of the termination, the date of the breach of an agreement for severance pay under Section 4(c), or the date the employee learns or should have learned of the facts forming the basis of the claim, whichever is latest. The time for filing is suspended while the employee is pursuing the employer's internal remedies and has not been notified in writing by the employer that the internal procedures have been concluded. Resort to an employer's internal procedures is not a condition for filing a complaint under this [Act].

(b) Except when an employee quits, an employer, within 10 business days after a termination, shall mail or deliver to the terminated employee a written statement of the reasons for the termination and a copy of this [Act] or a summary approved by the [Commission; Department; Service].

(c) An employer may file a complaint and demand for arbitration under this [Act] with the [Commission; Department; Service] to determine whether there is good cause for the termination of a named employee. At least 15 business days before filing, the employer shall mail or deliver to the employee a written statement of the employer's intention to file and the factors alleged to constitute good cause for a termination.

(d) The [Commission; Department; Service] shall promptly mail or deliver to the respondent a copy of the complaint and demand for arbitration. Within 21 days after receipt of a complaint, the respondent must file an answer with the [Commission; Department; Service] and mail a copy of the answer to the complainant. The answer of a respondent employer must include a copy of the statement of the reasons for the termination furnished the employee.

[(e) When a complaint is filed, a complainant employee or employer shall pay a filing fee to the [Commission; Department; Service] in [the amount of $_____] [an amount not exceeding the maximum filing fee for a civil action in the courts of general jurisdiction of this State]. The [Commission; Department; Service] may waive or defer payment of the filing fee upon a showing of the complainant employee's indigency.]

§ 6. Arbitration; Selection and Powers of Arbitrator; Hearings; Burden of Proof.

(a) Except as otherwise provided in this [Act], the [Uniform Arbitration Act] [_____ arbitration act of this State] applies to proceedings under this [Act] as if the parties had agreed to arbitrate under that statute. The [Commission; Department; Service] shall adopt procedural rules to regulate arbitration under this [Act]. The [Administrative Procedure Act and other] statutes of this State applicable to the procedures of state agencies do not apply to arbitration under this [Act].

(b) The [Commission; Department; Service] shall adopt rules specifying the qualifications, method of selection, and appointment of arbitrators. An arbitrator serving under this [Act] exercises the authority of the state.

(c) Subject to rules adopted by the [Commission; Department; Service], all forms of discovery [provided by applicable state statute, rule, or regulation] are available in the discretion of the arbitrator, who shall ensure there is no undue delay, expense, or inconvenience. Upon request, the employer shall provide the complainant or respondent employee a complete copy of the employee's personnel file.

(d) A party may be represented in arbitration by an attorney or other person authorized under the laws of this State to represent an individual in arbitration.

(e) A complainant employee has the burden of proving that a termination was without good cause or that an employer breached an agreement for severance pay under Section 4(c). A complainant employer has the burden of proving that there is good cause for a termination. In all arbitrations, the employer shall present its case first unless the employee alleges that a quitting or retirement was a termination within the meaning of Section 1(8)(iii).

(f) If an employee establishes that a termination was motivated in part by impermissible grounds, the employer, to avoid liability, must establish by a preponderance of the evidence that it would have terminated the employment even in the absence of the impermissible grounds.

§ 7. Awards.

(a) Within 30 days after the close of an arbitration hearing or at a later time agreeable to the parties, the arbitrator shall mail or deliver to the parties a written award sustaining or dismissing the complaint, in whole or in part, and specifying appropriate remedies, if any.

(b) An arbitrator may make one or more of the following awards for a termination in violation of this [Act]:

(1) reinstatement to the position of employment the employee held when employment was terminated or, if that is impractical, to a comparable position;

(2) full or partial backpay and reimbursement for lost fringe benefits, with interest, reduced by interim earnings from employment elsewhere, benefits received, and amounts that could have been received with reasonable diligence;

(3) if reinstatement is not awarded, a lump-sum severance payment at the employee's rate of pay in effect before the termination, for a period not exceeding [36 months] after the date of the award, together with the value of fringe benefits lost during that period, reduced by likely earnings and benefits from employment elsewhere, and taking into account such equitable considerations as the employee's length of service with the employer and the reasons for the termination; and

(4) reasonable attorney's fees and costs.

(c) An arbitrator may make either or both of the following awards for a violation of an agreement for severance pay under Section 4(c):

(1) enforcement of the severance pay and other applicable provisions of the agreement, with interest; and

(2) reasonable attorney's fees and costs.

(d) An arbitrator may not make an award except as provided in subsections (b) and (c). The arbitrator may not award damages for pain and suffering, emotional distress, defamation, fraud, or other injury under the common law; punitive damages; compensatory damages; or any other monetary award. In making a monetary award under this section, the arbitrator shall reduce the award by the amount of any monetary award to the employee in another forum for the same conduct of the employer. In making an award, the arbitrator is subject to the rules of issue, fact, and judgment preclusion applicable in courts of record in this State.

(e) If an arbitrator dismisses an employee's complaint and finds it frivolous, unreasonable, or without foundation, the arbitrator may award reasonable attorney's fees and costs to the prevailing employer.

(f) An arbitrator may sustain an employer's complaint and make an award declaring that there is good cause for the termination of a named employee. If the arbitrator dismisses the employer's complaint, the arbitrator may award reasonable attorney's fees and costs to the prevailing employee.

§ 8. Judicial Review and Enforcement.

(a) Either party to an arbitration may seek vacation, modification, or enforcement of the arbitrator's award in the [court of general jurisdiction] for the [county] in which the termination occurred or in which the employee resides.

(b) An application for vacation or modification must be filed within [90] days after issuance of the arbitrator's award. An application for enforcement may be filed at any time after issuance of the arbitrator's award.

(c) The court may vacate or modify an arbitrator's award only if the court finds that:

(1) the award was procured by corruption, fraud, or other improper means;

(2) there was evident partiality by the arbitrator or misconduct prejudicing the rights of a party;

(3) the arbitrator exceeded the powers of an arbitrator;

(4) the arbitrator committed a prejudicial error of law; or

(5) another ground exists for vacating the award under the [Uniform Arbitration Act] [_____ arbitration act of this State].

(d) In an application for vacation, modification, or enforcement of an arbitrator's award, the court may award a prevailing employee reasonable attorney's fees and costs. In an application by an employee for vacation of an arbitrator's award, the court may award a prevailing employer reasonable attorney's fees and costs if the court finds the employee's application is frivolous, unreasonable, or without foundation.

§ 9. Posting.

An employer shall post a copy of this [Act] or a summary approved by the [Commission; Department; Service] in a prominent place in the work area. An employer who violates this section is subject to a civil penalty not exceeding [$_____]. The [Attorney General] may bring a civil action, on behalf of this State, to impose and collect any civil penalty arising under this section.

§ 10. Retaliation Prohibited and Civil Action Created.

An employer or other employing person may not directly or indirectly take adverse action in retaliation against an individual for filing a complaint, giving testimony, or otherwise lawfully participating in proceedings under this [Act], whether or not the individual is an employee having rights under this [Act]. An employer or other employing person who violates this section is liable to the individual subjected to the adverse action in retaliation for damage caused by the action, punitive damages when appropriate, and reasonable attorney's fees. A separate civil action may be brought to enforce this liability. The employer is also subject to applicable procedures and remedies provided by Sections 5 through 8. . . .

MONTANA WRONGFUL DISCHARGE FROM EMPLOYMENT ACT OF 1987

Mont. Rev. Stat. §§ 39–2–901 to 39–2–915, as amended

§ 39–2–901. Short title

This part may be cited as the "Wrongful Discharge From Employment Act".

§ 39–2–902. Purpose

This part sets forth certain rights and remedies with respect to wrongful discharge. Except as provided in 39–2–912, this part provides the exclusive remedy for a wrongful discharge from employment.

§ 39–2–903. Definitions

In this part, the following definitions apply:

(1) "Constructive discharge" means the voluntary termination of employment by an employee because of a situation created by an act or omission of the employer which an objective, reasonable person would find so intolerable that voluntary termination is the only reasonable alternative. Constructive discharge does not mean voluntary termination because of an employer's refusal to promote the employee or improve wages, responsibilities, or other terms and conditions of employment.

(2) "Discharge" includes a constructive discharge as defined in subsection (1) and any other termination of employment, including resignation, elimination of the job, layoff for lack of work, failure to recall or rehire, and any other cutback in the number of employees for a legitimate business reason.

(3) "Employee" means a person who works for another for hire. Tho term does not include a person who is an independent contractor.

(4) "Fringe benefits" means the value of any employer-paid vacation leave, sick leave, medical insurance plan, disability insurance plan, life insurance plan, and pension benefit plan in force on the date of the termination.

(5) "Good cause" means reasonable job-related grounds for dismissal based on a failure to satisfactorily perform job duties, disruption of the employer's operation, or other legitimate business reason. The legal use of a lawful product by an individual off the employer's premises during nonworking hours is not a legitimate business reason, unless the employer acts within the provisions of 39–2–313(3) or (4).

(6) "Lost wages" means the gross amount of wages that would have been reported to the internal revenue service as gross income on Form W–2

and includes additional compensation deferred at the option of the employee.

(7) "Public policy" means a policy in effect at the time of the discharge concerning the public health, safety, or welfare established by constitutional provision, statute, or administrative rule.

§ 39–2–904. Elements of wrongful discharge—presumptive probationary period

(1) A discharge is wrongful only if:

(a) it was in retaliation for the employee's refusal to violate public policy or for reporting a violation of public policy;

(b) the discharge was not for good cause and the employee had completed the employer's probationary period of employment; or

(c) the employer violated the express provisions of its own written personnel policy.

(2) (a) During a probationary period of employment, the employment may be terminated at the will of either the employer or the employee on notice to the other for any reason or for no reason.

(b) If an employer does not establish a specific probationary period or provide that there is no probationary period prior to or at the time of hire, there is a probationary period of 6 months from the date of hire.

§ 39–2–905. Remedies

(1) If an employer has committed a wrongful discharge, the employee may be awarded lost wages and fringe benefits for a period not to exceed 4 years from the date of discharge, together with interest thereon. Interim earnings, including amounts the employee could have earned with reasonable diligence, must be deducted from the amount awarded for lost wages. Before interim earnings are deducted from lost wages, there must be deducted from the interim earnings any reasonable amounts expended by the employee in searching for, obtaining, or relocating to new employment.

(2) The employee may recover punitive damages otherwise allowed by law if it is established by clear and convincing evidence that the employer engaged in actual fraud or actual malice in the discharge of the employee in violation of 39–2–904(1)(a).

(3) There is no right under any legal theory to damages for wrongful discharge under this part for pain and suffering, emotional distress, compensatory damages, punitive damages, or any other form of damages, except as provided for in subsections (1) and (2).

(§§ 39–2–906 through 39–2–910 reserved.)

§ 39–2–911. Limitation of actions

(1) An action under this part must be filed within 1 year after the date of discharge.

(2) If an employer maintains written internal procedures, other than those specified in 39–2–912, under which an employee may appeal a discharge within the organizational structure of the employer, the employee shall first exhaust those procedures prior to filing an action under this part. The employee's failure to initiate or exhaust available internal procedures is a defense to an action brought under this part. If the employer's internal procedures are not completed within 90 days from the date the employee initiates the internal procedures, the employee may file an action under this part and for purposes of this subsection the employer's internal procedures are considered exhausted. The limitation period in subsection (1) is tolled until the procedures are exhausted. In no case may the provisions of the employer's internal procedures extend the limitation period in subsection (1) more than 120 days.

(3) If the employer maintains written internal procedures under which an employee may appeal a discharge within the organizational structure of the employer, the employer shall within 7 days of the date of the discharge notify the discharged employee of the existence of such procedures and shall supply the discharged employee with a copy of them. If the employer fails to comply with this subsection, the discharged employee need not comply with subsection (2).

§ 39–2–912. Exemptions

This part does not apply to a discharge:

(1) that is subject to any other state or federal statute that provides a procedure or remedy for contesting the dispute. The statutes include those that prohibit discharge for filing complaints, charges, or claims with administrative bodies or that prohibit unlawful discrimination based on race, national origin, sex, age, disability, creed, religion, political belief, color, marital status, and other similar grounds.

(2) of an employee covered by a written collective bargaining agreement or a written contract of employment for a specific term.

§ 39–2–913. Preemption of common-law remedies

Except as provided in this part, no claim for discharge may arise from tort or express or implied contract.

§ 39–2–914. Arbitration

(1) A party may make a written offer to arbitrate a dispute that otherwise could be adjudicated under this part.

(2) An offer to arbitrate must be in writing and contain the following provisions:

(a) A neutral arbitrator must be selected by mutual agreement or, in the absence of agreement, as provided in 27–5–211.

(b) The arbitration must be governed by the Uniform Arbitration Act, Title 27, chapter 5. If there is a conflict between the Uniform Arbitration Act and this part, this part applies.

(c) The arbitrator is bound by this part.

(3) If a complaint is filed under this part, the offer to arbitrate must be made within 60 days after service of the complaint and must be accepted in writing within 30 days after the date the offer is made.

(4) A discharged employee who makes a valid offer to arbitrate that is accepted by the employer and who prevails in such arbitration is entitled to have the arbitrator's fee and all costs of arbitration paid by the employer.

(5) If a valid offer to arbitrate is made and accepted, arbitration is the exclusive remedy for the wrongful discharge dispute and there is no right to bring or continue a lawsuit under this part. The arbitrator's award is final and binding, subject to review of the arbitrator's decision under the provisions of the Uniform Arbitration Act.

§ 39–2–915. Effect of rejection of offer to arbitrate

A party who makes a valid offer to arbitrate that is not accepted by the other party and who prevails in an action under this part is entitled as an element of costs to reasonable attorney fees incurred subsequent to the date of the offer.

SAMPLE COLLECTIVE–BARGAINING AGREEMENT

LABOR AGREEMENT

An exclusive representative for the purpose of collective bargaining having been designated, this Agreement is made and entered in this 1st day of January, 2005, by and between the ABC Company (hereinafter "Company") and the United Workers International Union and its Local No. 100 (hereinafter "Union").

PREAMBLE AND PURPOSE

The Company and the Union desire orderly and peaceful relations with the employees covered by this Agreement, and they seek to achieve the highest level of employee performance consistent with safety, good health, and sustained effort. The purpose of this Agreement is to set forth terms and conditions of employment, to prevent interruptions of work and interferences with the efficient operation of the Company's business, to secure fair and prompt disposition of grievances, and generally to promote sound and cooperative labor-management relations.

ARTICLE 1. RECOGNITION, UNION SECURITY, REPRESENTATION

§ 1. **Recognition**. The Company recognizes the Union as the sole collective-bargaining agency for all warehouse and production and maintenance employees, excluding all guards, professional and technical employees, office clerical employees and supervisors as defined in the Labor–Management Relations Act, 1947, as amended.

§ 2. **Union Security**. (A) Each employee who as of the date of signing of this Agreement is a member of the Union in good standing in accordance with the constitution and by-laws of the Union shall, as a condition of continued employment by the Company, maintain membership in the Union during the term of this Agreement to the extent of tendering the periodic dues uniformly required as a condition of retaining membership in the Union.

(B) Each employee who is not a member of the Union on the date of signing of this Agreement, and each employee who is hired on or after said date, shall, as a condition of continued employment by the Company, become a member of the Union on the thirtieth (30th) day following the date of signing of this Agreement or the date of their employment, whichever is later, and maintain membership in the Union during the term of this Agreement to the extent of tendering the initiation fee and periodic dues uniformly required as a condition of acquiring or retaining membership in the Union.

(C) The Company will discharge any employee who fails to satisfy the fee or dues obligations imposed by paragraphs (A) and (B) above, within ten

(10) days after receipt of written notice from the Union that such employee is delinquent in such obligations.

(D) Employees who are not signatory members of the Union, but who tender to the Union the fee or dues required by this Agreement, and who object to the Union's expenditure of periodic dues money for political or ideological purposes unrelated to collective bargaining or the administration of this Agreement, may notify the Union in writing of their objection and request a pro-rata reduction in their periodic dues payment in direct proportion to the amount of money being expended for such unrelated purposes.

§ 3.   Checkoff. Upon receipt of a lawfully executed written authorization from an employee, the Company agrees for the term of this Agreement, or until such authorization is revoked in accordance with its terms, to deduct initiation fees and the regular monthly Union membership dues of such employee from the employee's first pay of each month, or succeeding pay in such month, if necessary, and promptly to remit such deduction to the official designated by the Union in writing to receive such deductions. The Union will notify the Company in writing of the exact amount of such initiation fee or regular monthly membership dues to be deducted. The authorizations provided for by this Section shall conform to all applicable Federal and State laws.

§ 4.   Union Stewards. The Union shall have the right to appoint up to four (4) Union Stewards to process grievances arising under this Agreement and to perform such other tasks the Union assigns, provided that such activities shall not interfere with the Company's business operations or with the performance of the Steward's regular job duties. Stewards shall at all times notify the Shift Superintendent before leaving their jobsites to perform grievance or other Union business.

§ 5.   Plant Closing and Relocation. If the Company plans a shutdown of its operation at its present location and a move to another location, it will, if practicable to do so, attempt to give the Union at least three months' notice of its plans prior to the actual shutdown and move, and will, in addition to giving such notice, negotiate with the Union concerning the impact on employees as a result of such a shutdown and move.

§ 6.   No Discrimination. In regard to hiring, tenure of employment, or any condition of employment, the Company shall not discriminate against any employee because of membership in, or lawful activities on behalf of, the Union, or because of race, color, sex, religion, or national origin. Nor shall the Union discriminate against any employee for such reasons.

ARTICLE II. MANAGEMENT RIGHTS

It is agreed that the management of the business and the direction of the working forces, including, but not limited to, the right to plan, direct and control operations; to determine the operations or services to be performed in or at the plant or by employees of the Company; to schedule the working hours; to hire, promote, demote and transfer, to suspend, discipline, discharge for just cause, or to relieve employees because of lack of work or for other legitimate reasons; to make and enforce reasonable shop rules and regulations not inconsistent with the provisions of this Agreement; to introduce new and improved methods, materials or facilities, or to change existing methods, materials or facilities; are vested exclusively in the Company; provided, however, that such rights shall not be exercised in any manner violative of any of the provisions of this Agreement.

ARTICLE III. HOURS OF WORK; OVERTIME

It is understood that the provisions of this Article do not constitute a guarantee of hours of work per day or per week. It is further understood that there shall be no pyramiding of overtime premiums, and that overtime shall not be paid more than once for the same hours worked.

§ 1. Work Day and Work Week. The work week for payroll purposes shall be a seven (7) consecutive day period commencing at 12:01 AM on Monday and ending at 12:00 midnight on the following Sunday. A work day shall be the twenty-four (24) hour period commencing with the employee's scheduled starting time. The normal work days shall be five (5), Monday through Friday, inclusive. The normal working hours per day shall be eight (8), exclusive of a lunch period, and the normal working hours per week shall be forty (40). The normal starting time for the first shift, second shift, and third shift shall be 7:15 A.M., 3:45 P.M., and 11:45 P.M., respectively.

§ 2. Overtime Premium. Overtime premium shall be paid as follows:

(a) For all hours worked in excess of eight (8) hours worked in any one day time and one-half (1½) of the straight time hourly rate.

(b) For all hours worked in excess of forty (40) hours worked in a work week—time and one-half (1½) of the straight time hourly rate.

(c) For all hours worked on Saturday, except when such hours are part of the regularly scheduled third shift commencing on Friday and carrying over into Saturday—time and one-half (1½) of the straight time hourly rate.

(d) For all hours worked on Sundays, except when such hours are part of the regularly scheduled third shift commencing on Saturday and carrying over into Sunday—two (2) times the straight time hourly rate.

(e) For all hours worked on holidays, except when such hours are part of the regularly scheduled third shift commencing on the day prior to the holiday and carrying over into the holiday—two (2) times the straight time hourly rate.

§ 3. Allocation of Overtime Opportunities. The Company shall rotate overtime opportunities among qualified employees who normally perform the work that is being assigned for overtime. The company agrees to make available for examination by the Union Steward a record of overtime assignments. If it is determined that any employee has not been given a fair share of overtime opportunities, the employee shall be given preference for future overtime assignments until the imbalance is corrected.

§ **4.** **Reporting Time**. Employees who report for work at the regular starting time, and who have not been notified not to report, shall be guaranteed four (4) hours of work or pay for four (4) hours at the regular hourly rate. This guarantee shall not apply where the failure to provide work results from emergencies beyond the control of the Company, such as work stoppages, accidents, fires, storms, floods, power failures, or other similar occurrences.

ARTICLE IV. WAGES

Effective January 1, 2005, and for the period of this Agreement, employees working under this Agreement shall be paid the wage rates set forth in the attached schedule of wages and job classifications hereby made a part of this Agreement, as Appendix "A." All employees shall be paid their pay weekly.

§ **1.** **Wage Increases**. Effective July 1, 2005, there shall be a wage increase for all covered employees of eighty-nine cents (89¢) per hour. Effective July 1, 2006, there shall be a wage increase of ninety-five cents (95¢) per hour for all covered employees. These increases shall be granted across the board to all employees holding job classifications described in attached Appendix "A."

§ **2.** **Temporary Transfers**. Temporary transfers of employees from one job classification to another or from one department to another may be made from time to time as business needs require. A temporary transfer will not exceed four (4) consecutive weeks in duration unless agreed to by the parties.

Any employee who is temporarily transferred to work outside his/her regular classification for in excess of one (1) work day shall be paid his/her regular hourly rate or the starting rate of the classification to which he/she is assigned, whichever is higher; however, the employee may be paid a higher rate if, in the judgment of the Company, the employee's ability warrants it. Any employee so transferred for one (1) work day or less shall continue to receive he/she regular hourly rate.

If employees are to be temporarily transferred from their job, the most senior employees shall be assigned to the most desirable vacancies that he Company wishes to fill on a temporary basis, providing said employees have the ability to perform the assigned work.

Any employee who is temporarily assigned or transferred to another classification at his/her request because of inability to perform his/her regular work, or an employee who is permanently transferred to another classification, or an employee who is transferred to another classification in lieu of layoff pursuant to the Seniority Article, shall receive the starting rate of the classification provided that he/she may be paid a higher rate if, in the judgment of the Company, the employee's ability warrants it.

§ 3. Shift Premium. All employees working on the night shift shall receive, in cents per hour, ten percent (10%) of other straight time hourly rate. "Employees working on the night shift" is hereby defined as employees who are scheduled to and commence work on a shift for which the starting time is at or after 12:00 o'clock noon and before 4:00 A.M.

§ 4. Rest Periods. Employees shall receive a ten (10) minute rest period for each four (4) hours worked without any reduction in pay. Said rest period shall be staggered by the Company.

ARTICLE V. VACATIONS

§ 1. Amount. Full time eligible employees shall be entitled each calendar year to a vacation with pay in accord with one of the following provisions:

(a) All employees who on June 1st have been employed by the Company six (6) months or more shall be granted one (1) week's vacation with pay.

(b) All employees who have continuous service of two (2) years but less than ten (10) years as of the anniversary date of their employment shall be granted two (2) weeks' vacation with pay.

(c) All employees who have continuous service of ten (10) years or more as of the anniversary date of their employment shall be granted three (3) weeks' vacation with pay.

(d) All employees who have continuous service of twenty (20) years or more as of the anniversary date of their employment shall be granted four (4) weeks' vacation with pay.

Vacation pay shall be computed at the employee's straight time hourly rate as of June 1st of the year in which the vacation is to be taken (including the night shift premium for the employee who is regularly working on the night shift at the time the vacation commences) based on a forty (40) hour week.

§ 2. Eligibility. To be eligible for vacation benefits, as outlined above, an employee must be a full-time employee who:

(a) to be eligible for benefits under Section 1(a) of this Article, must have worked at least 1600 hours during the twelve (12) month period prior to June 1st of the year in which the vacation is to be taken. If an employee has worked six (6) months but less than twelve (12) months as of June 1st, said employee shall be eligible for a vacation if the employee has worked the same prorated share hours during employment as is based on the ratio of 4:5.

(b) to be eligible for benefits as described under Section 1(b), 1(c) or 1(d) of this Article, must have worked at least 1600 hours during the twelve (12) month period prior to June 1st of the year in which the vacation is to be taken. If an employee works between 1000 hours and 1600 hours, vacation benefits will be prorated on the basis of the "hours worked" constituting the numerator and "1600" acting as the denominator (e.g., if an employee works 1200 hours, the employee receives 1200 ÷ 1600 of vacation benefits, or 75%).

In computing the number of hours worked under this Section, credit shall be given for holidays (eight (8) hours), prior year's vacation (forty (40) hours per week), straight time hours lost on death leave or while serving on jury duty.

§ 3. Vacation Schedules. The time allotted to an employee for a vacation will be established by the Company and the vacation period will be such as will cause a minimum interference with Company operations. Every employee eligible for vacation pay will be notified of the assigned date of vacation as far in advance as possible, and wherever possible employees will be given preference as to the time of their vacation on the basis of seniority. The Company reserves the right to shut down its plant so that all vacations may be taken at one and the same time. In case of a shutdown for vacation purposes, the company will give reasonable notice to the Union and the employees.

ARTICLE VI. HOLIDAYS

§ 1. Holidays Observed. The following days shall be considered holidays: New Year's Day, Martin Luther King, Jr. Day, Memorial Day, Independence Day, Labor Day, Thanksgiving Day, Christmas Eve (4 hours), Christmas Day, New Year's Eve (4 hours). Holidays will be observed on the day of their occurrence, except that when a holiday falls on Sunday and is observed on Monday by the State or Federal Governments, it shall be observed on such Monday.

§ 2. Holiday Pay and Eligibility. Employees shall be paid eight (8) hours' straight time pay for holidays not worked provided they meet all of the following eligibility requirements:

(a) The employee has completed the probationary period;

(b) The employee worked the regularly scheduled hours on the last scheduled work day prior to and on the employee's next scheduled work day after the holiday, except where the employee has a reasonable excuse for being unable to work on the scheduled work day; and

(c) The employee performed work during the week in which the holiday falls.

An employee shall not be eligible for holiday pay if the employee is scheduled to work on the holiday and fails to work the scheduled hours on the holiday. An employee who worked the scheduled hours on a holiday shall receive holiday pay in addition to pay for the hours worked provided for in Section 3(d) of Article III. If a holiday falls within an eligible employee's vacation period, the employee shall be paid holiday pay in addition to vacation pay, if any. Holidays falling within the normal work week (Monday through Friday) shall be considered as time worked (eight (8) hours) in computing overtime.

ARTICLE VII. LEAVES OF ABSENCE

Employees shall have the right to make, in writing, application for leaves of absence for justifiable reasons. The Company shall have the sole right to determine whether or not the leaves shall be granted and the duration of any leave. Original leaves of absence will not be granted for a period to exceed six (6) months except that a leave of absence for pregnancy will be six (6) months. Leaves of absence shall be without pay and may be renewed upon written request showing good cause. Seniority shall accumulate during authorized leaves. Any employee misrepresenting reasons for requesting leave of absence, or who engages in other employment while on authorized leave, shall be subject to discharge.

ARTICLE VIII. SENIORITY

§ 1. **Probationary Period**. Seniority is defined as an employee's length of continuous service with the Company in years, months and days dating from the last date of hire. A new employee is subject to the provisions of this Agreement but shall be considered a probationary employee for the first thirty (30) days of continuous employment, after which the employee's seniority shall date back to the date of hire. Probationary employees shall not have seniority and may be laid off, discharged, or otherwise terminated by the Company, and such action shall not be subject to the grievance procedure of this Agreement.

§ 2. **Seniority Standard**. In all applications of seniority under this Agreement, where ability to perform the available work is relatively equal, seniority shall be the determining factor. The Company shall evaluate and determine the employee's ability, subject to the right of an employee to file a grievance challenging the Company's evaluation and determination of said factor. The Company shall give the Union a current seniority list and shall notify the Union of any changes in said list.

§ 3. **Layoff and Recall**. In the event of a reduction in the workforce, the following procedure shall be followed: (a) Any employees working in the General Laborer Classification with less than two (2) years' seniority shall first be laid off from the plant, provided that the remaining employees possess sufficient ability to perform the work. (b) If a further reduction is to be made, those employees will be displaced from the affected classification according to the test set forth in § 2 of this Article. Employees so displaced shall be given an opportunity by the Company to perform the job of an employee (if any) with less seniority within the displaced employee's department, in accord with the test set forth in § 2 of this Article. Employees who are finally displaced from the department under this procedure shall then be given an opportunity to perform the job of an employee (if any) in another department in accord with the test set forth in § 2 of this Article. No employee will be transferred to a higher rated job under the provisions of this Section. In the event of an increase in the workforce following a reduction, laid off employees shall be recalled to their regular classification according to the test as set forth in § 2 of this Article.

§ 4. **Job Posting and Bidding**. In the event that a permanent job vacancy develops in a classification other than General Laborer and covered by this Agreement, notice of such vacancy shall be posted for a period of two (2) work days, during which seniority employees in lower-rated classifications desiring promotion to such vacancy may apply therefor on forms furnished by the Company and available to employees on request. As between such employees where ability is relatively equal, primary consideration shall be given to seniority.

Nothing contained in this Section shall prevent the Company from temporarily filling a posted vacancy until it is determined whether there are applicants with the ability to perform satisfactorily the work involved, or from offering the posted vacancy to a qualified employee who did not apply, or hiring a new qualified employee for a vacancy if there are no applicants during the period of posting, or if none of the applicants has the ability to perform satisfactorily the work involved. Any employee accepting a promotion pursuant to this Section may not bid on any other posted job within one (1) year following his/her promotion.

Any employee who accepts a promotion in accordance with the provisions of this Section and fails to demonstrate an ability to perform the work involved in a satisfactory manner shall be retransferred to the job classification from which he/she was promoted, displacing the employee, if any, who replaced him/her, without loss of seniority; provided, however, that no such employee may therefore apply for any other posted vacancy in the same job classification.

§ 5. **Retention of Seniority out of Bargaining Unit.** An employee transferred out of the bargaining unit to another position with the Company shall, upon subsequent transfer back into the bargaining unit within six (6) months, retain the seniority which he/she had at the time of transfer out of the bargaining unit. In all other cases, employees transferred out of the bargaining unit shall lose the seniority they had at the time of such transfer after they have been out of the bargaining unit for more than six (6) months.

§ 6. **Termination of Seniority**. Seniority and the employment relationship shall be broken and terminated when an employee: (a) quits; (b) is discharged for cause; (c) is absent for three (3) consecutive work days without notifying the company; (d) fails to report for work after a layoff within five (5) work days after a written notice of recall is sent by the Company by certified mail, return receipt requested, to the employee at his/her last address of record on file with the Company; or (e) is laid off for one (1) year (in the case of employees with more than one (1) year's seniority at time of layoff) or for one-half (½) the employee's seniority (in the case of employees with less than one (1) year's seniority at time of layoff).

ARTICLE IX. GRIEVANCE–ARBITRATION PROCEDURE

A diligent effort shall be made to settle all grievances as soon as possible after they have been presented. It is the desire of the Company and the Union that the investigation and discussion of grievances will be conducted in a manner which maximizes fairness to employees and minimizes lost time and production. However, grievances may be investigated by Union and Company representatives during working hours.

§ 1. Adjustment of Grievances. A "grievance," under this Agreement, is any dispute or difference of opinion between the Company and the Union or between the Company and any employee(s) covered by this Agreement involving the meaning, interpretation, an application of the provisions of this Agreement, except for an alleged violation of Article X of this Agreement, it being understood that this Article IX shall not be applicable at all to said Article X. Grievances shall be handled as follows:

Step 1: Plant Superintendent. Any employee who believes he/she has a grievance shall discuss it with the Plant Superintendent either alone or accompanied by the immediate supervisor and the Union Steward as the employee may desire. The Plant Superintendent shall give an answer to the Steward and the grievant within one (1) day after such discussion.

Step 2: Plant Manager. If the grievance is not settled in Step 1 and the employee or Union desires to appeal, the Union's business agent shall appeal in writing to the Plant Manager within five (5) days after the designated Plant Superintendent's answer in Step 1. A meeting between the Plant Manager, a Union official and the Union Steward shall be held at a mutually agreeable time. If the grievance is settled as a result of such meeting, the settlement shall be reduced to writing and signed by the Company Plant Manager and the official of the Union who participated in the Second Step meeting. If no settlement is reached, the Plant Manager shall give the Company's written answer to the same Union official within five (5) days following their meeting.

Step 3: Arbitration. If the grievance is not settled in Step 2 and the Company's final answer is not satisfactory to the Union, the Union may appeal the grievance to arbitration by giving written notice of its desire to arbitrate to the Plant Manager within ten (10) days after the date of the Company's final answer in Step 2. If the grievance is appealed to arbitration, representatives of the Company and the Union shall meet to select an arbitrator. If the parties are unable to agree on an arbitrator within ten (10) work days after the Union has served its written notice upon the Company, the parties shall request the American Arbitration Ass'n to submit a list of five (5) arbitrators. The party requesting arbitration shall then strike two (2) names from the list and the other party shall then strike two (2). The person whose name remains shall be the arbitrator. The arbitrator shall be notified of his selection by a joint letter from the Company and the Union requesting that he set a time and place for the hearing, subject to availability of the Company and Union representatives, and the letter shall specify the issue(s) in dispute to the arbitrator.

§ 2. **Authority of Arbitrator**. The arbitrator shall have no right to amend, modify, nullify, ignore or add to the provisions of this Agreement. He shall consider and decide only the particular issue(s) presented to him in writing by the Company and the union, and his decision and award shall be based solely upon his interpretation of the meaning or application of the terms of this Agreement to the facts of the grievance presented. If the matter sought to be arbitrated does not involve an interpretation of the terms or provisions of this Agreement, the arbitrator shall so rule in his award and the matter shall not be further entertained by the arbitrator. The award of the arbitrator shall be final and binding on the Company, the Union, and the employee or employees involved. The expenses of the arbitrator, including his fee, shall be shared equally by the Company and the Union.

§ 3. **Time Limit for Filing Grievances**. No grievance shall be entertained or processed unless it is submitted to the Company within fifteen (15) days after occurrence of the event giving rise to the grievance or after the Union or affected employee(s) acquired knowledge of the occurrence of such event. Any Company liability will only commence to accrue as of the time of the filing of the grievance.

ARTICLE X. NO STRIKE OR LOCKOUT

The Company and the Union agree that the grievance and arbitration procedures provided herein shall be the sole and exclusive means of resolving all grievances arising under the terms of this Agreement, and, further, that remedies and procedures provided by statute shall be the sole and exclusive means of settling all other disputes between the employees and the Company or between the Union and the Company. Accordingly, neither the Union nor the employees will instigate, promote, sponsor, engage in, or condone any strike, slowdown, concerted stoppage of work or any other intentional interruption of work over any dispute involving the interpretation or application of this Agreement or over any other dispute. In the event that any employee or group of employees covered by this Agreement shall, during its term, participate or engage in any of the activities herein prohibited, the Union agrees, immediately upon being notified by the Company, to direct such employee or group of employees, in writing, to cease such activity and resume work at once. The Company shall have the right to discharge or otherwise discipline any employee who engages in any of the activities prohibited by this Article, and, in the event a grievance is filed, the sole question for arbitration shall be whether the employee engaged in the prohibited activity. During the term of this Agreement, the Company agrees that it will not institute a lockout.

ARTICLE XI. EMPLOYEE BENEFITS

The Company agrees that, effective January 1, 2005, and during the term of this Agreement, it shall continue in effect the Medical Insurance, Dental Insurance, Life Insurance, and Pension Plan programs described in Appendix "B" attached hereto, which Appendix "B" is hereby made a part of this Agreement. The formulas for determining the weekly or monthly sums of money the Company shall contribute for each employee who has been on the payroll thirty (30) days or more, and who is covered by and eligible for benefits under said employee-benefit Programs, are designated in said Appendix "B."

If an employee is absent because of illness or off-the-job injury and notifies the Company of such absence, the Company shall continue to make the required employee-benefit contributions for such employee for a period of four (4) weeks. If an employee is injured on the job, the Company shall continue to pay the required contributions until such employee returns to work; however, such contributions shall not be paid for a period of more than six (6) months. If an employee is granted a leave of absence, the Company shall collect from said employee, prior to the leave of absence being effective, sufficient monies to pay the required contributions into the said employee-benefit Programs during the period of absence.

ARTICLE XII. GENERAL

§ 1. **Bulletin Boards**. The Company agrees to provide a bulletin board and space on same for the Union to keep its members informed concerning Union meetings, elections, recreational events, and social affairs. No notices shall be posted without prior submission to the Company's Personnel Manager.

§ 2. **Safety and Health**. The Company shall make reasonable provisions for the safety and health of its employees in its plant during the hours of their employment. Under no circumstances shall an employee be required or assigned to engage in any activity in violation of any applicable statute, court order, or government regulation relating to the safety of person or equipment.

§ 3. **Work by Non–Bargaining Unit Employees**. Employees who are not in the bargaining unit may perform bargaining unit work in cases of absenteeism, emergency training of employees, and in accordance with practices existing prior to the date of this Agreement; or where the performance of the work does not result in the loss of overtime to bargaining unit employees.

§ 4. **Union Activity During Working Hours**. The Union agrees that its members will not carry on Union activities in the plant or on

Company premises during working hours. The lunch period and authorized breaks shall not be deemed working hours.

§ 5. Jury Duty. Employees whose absence is necessitated by jury duty will be paid the difference between their jury pay and the regular straight time earnings up to eight (8) hours for each day they would have received had they worked.

§ 6. Death Leave. In the case of the death of an employee's mother, father, sister, brother, spouse, or child, the Company will grant up to three (3) days' leave with pay to the employee in order to attend the funeral. This death leave will be extended to five (5) days for an employee attending a funeral being held five hundred (500) miles or more from the location of the plant. In the case of the death of an employee's mother-in-law or father-in-law, the Company will grant one (1) day's leave with pay in order to attend the funeral.

§ 7. Election Day Pay. An employee who has registered and is entitled to vote at a national election shall, on the day of the election, be granted one (1) hour's excused absence with pay.

ARTICLE XIII. COMPLETE AGREEMENT

This Agreement shall constitute the entire Agreement between the parties and concludes collective bargaining for its term. The parties acknowledge that, during the negotiations which resulted in this Agreement, each had the unlimited right and opportunity to make demands and proposals with respect to any subject or matter not removed by law from the area of collective bargaining, and that the understandings and Agreements arrived at by the parties after the exercise of the right and opportunity are set forth in this Agreement. Therefore, the parties hereto, for the life of this Agreement, each voluntarily and unqualifiedly waives the right, and each expressly agrees that the other shall not be obligated, to bargain collectively with respect to any subject or matter referred to, or covered or not specifically referred to or covered in the Agreement, even though such subject or matter may not have been within the knowledge or contemplation of either or both of the parties at the time that they negotiated or signed this Agreement.

ARTICLE XIV. TERMINATION OF AGREEMENT

This Agreement shall be in effect from January 1, 2005, to December 31, 2007, and from year to year thereafter unless either party gives written notice of its desire to terminate this Agreement at least sixty (60) days prior to December 31, 2007, or sixty (60) days prior to any subsequent anniversary date thereof.

IN WITNESS WHEREOF, the parties have set their hands and seals on the day and year first above written.

(Appendix "A," Job Classifications and Hourly Wage Rates, and Appendix "B," Employee–Benefit Programs, are omitted.)

†